D1706423

SMALL
TALK

How to Start a Conversation, Truly Connect with Others and Make a Killer First Impression

DIANE WESTON

Published by *Monkey Publishing*

Edited by *Lily Marlene Booth*

Cover Design by *Diogo Lando*

Printed by *Amazon*

ISBN (Print): 978-1095426906

ASIN (eBook): B07R1RCLVH

1st Edition, published in 2019

© 2019 by Monkey Publishing

Monkey Publishing

Lerchenstrasse 111

22767 Hamburg

Germany

Your Free Bonus

As a small token of thanks for buying this book, I am offering a free bonus guide, exclusively to my readers, about Emotional Intelligence and how it can improve your life.

Emotional Intelligence can play a big role to increase the quality of your relationships and thus the quality of your life. Research has shown that emotionally intelligent people are open to new experiences, can show feelings adequate to the situation, either good or bad, and find it easy to socialize with other people and establish new contacts. They handle stress well, realistically assess the achievements of themselves and others and are not afraid of constructive criticism and taking calculated risks.

The free bonus guide will provide some basic strategies on how to apply emotional intelligence to your everyday life. If you are curious you can download the free guide here: https://smalltalkbonus.gr8.com/

Content

Part 1

Small Talk Novice

Wow, nice weather we're having today," you say to the stranger who's standing next to you. "Yep, sure is," the person responds. And the silence lengthens.

A small talk nightmare — and one you've probably encountered before since you're reading this book. But it doesn't have to be like that. This book will explain all about it, why humans engage in small talk, what affects how well you succeed at it, and will give you tips and tricks to make you better at small talk so you can be better at life.

Why small talk?

Well, it turns out that small talk can actually have a big impact on your life and the lives of others. Just because you're only chit-chatting with someone, doesn't mean you're not connecting with that person. Small talk is sometimes denigrated by suggestions that it isn't deep — it's only superficial. But small talk, if done correctly, can allow you to connect in a meaningful way with the person at the grocery store checkout, or your partner or child.

Small talk is a necessary social skill that has evolved to turn people you don't know into people you do. It turns a stranger into an acquaintance or an acquaintance into a friend.

Small talk is a skill that can be learned. It is an ability that can actually bring you closer to, not only strangers you meet on an airplane or at a party, but also to the people you know best.

Perhaps with practice you will eventually become a small talk master. You know, the kind of person that you've only been talking to for a couple of minutes but who has already made you feel at ease.

Learning to be good at small talk means that you don't have to have any more awkward social encounters with people you don't know. By using exchanged words as a bridge between you and the other person, you can connect with them emotionally and form perhaps a weak social tie known as an acquaintance, or you may deepen a close relationship you already have with a friend or a partner.

The key to being good at small talk is to give attention to the other person without thinking about what you're going to say next. Giving attention is the most valuable gift you can give another person and will be discussed in more detail later.

What this book will teach you

In this book, you will learn how to master small talk. In the introduction, we will begin by understanding the basics of human interaction, communication, and why we speak to each other the way that we do. Once you understand the mechanics of small talk, in the second section we will get into preparing yourself for communicating and connecting with other people. The third part of the book will provide concrete techniques and methods for making small talk, as well as giving you some troubleshooting tips. At the end of the book, you will find some useful checklists to help when you are practicing and preparing for a social event. So, with that said, let's get started learning how to make small talk.

Basics of Human Interaction

Humans evolved social capacity as part of our evolution. The neocortex is the part of the brain that controls social interaction. When you compare the brains of primates with the brains of humans, you'll find that in humans the neocortex is far larger and more developed. We evolved to be social beings. And for good reason. One human is hard-pressed to fend off a wild animal, but a group of humans can easily defeat a wolf, bear, or lion.

Recently scientists have discovered that our need to connect is as fundamental as our need for food or water. Communication is what builds social bonds and is what connected primitive humans so that they could work together to protect themselves and their families. Modern humans need communication just as much — or perhaps even more in our supposedly disconnected era — in order to connect with others in work and play and also to build healthy relationships.

Introverts and Extroverts

There can be no discussion of small talk without touching upon the differences in communication styles between introverts and extroverts. Many people think that they understand the terms but there are a few myths that need clearing up.

The main difference between introverts and extroverts is where the person gets their energy from. An extrovert gets their energy from people and may feel depleted if they spend too much time alone. On the other hand, introverts recharge their energy when they spend time by themselves, and being around other people tends to reduce their energy reserves.

There are a few other differences in that, as a general rule, introverts like to have more time to think about things before they speak and extroverts tend to be quick in groups to formulate thoughts and express them. This has given a false impression that introverts sometimes don't have anything to say or are even mentally inferior. That is simply not true. Yes, often in a group, an introvert will barely speak. But if you give an introvert time or get them alone one-on-one, they will talk your ear off with all their ideas.

How does this affect our discussion on small talk? Well, it is good to know if you are an extrovert or an introvert. A quick search online will show you many quizzes that you can use to determine where you get your energy from. Knowing this, you can understand yourself better and the amount of effort it may take you to become good at small talk.

Also, it may be good to try and gauge your conversational partner so that you can adjust your communication style to take into account the other person's communication comfort level.

An extrovert, who in the past wasn't good at small talk, may have simply been talking too much about themselves or about subjects that turned off the person they were talking to. Whereas, an introvert, who in the past didn't do well with small talk, may have been unwilling to push past the discomfort of speaking with someone who they didn't know very well. We will deal with both sorts of challenges in the main part of this book.

Basics of Communication

We will now look at two different models of communication in order to understand how people communicate on a deep level. This will allow you to follow what's truly happening in the conversation beneath the words.

Four-Ear Model

We will look at Schulz von Thun's four-ear model of communication in order for you to get a better comprehension of why people say the things they say and to enable you to better understand your conversational partners. This will not be very technical, so don't worry, and it will give you a basis for making sense of your interactions with others, both in your deep relationships and on a more superficial level when making small talk with strangers.

Schulz von Thun's four-ear model of communication states that there are four levels of interaction. In any exchange between two people, there are the following four levels of a message: Factual information, the self-statement, the relationship indicator, and the appeal.

Here is a quick explanation of what each part means.

- Factual information - the bare content of the

message.

- The self-statement — this is the part of the message that shows something about the speaker.
- The relationship indicator of the message - tells the listener something about how the speaker feels about the person they're speaking to.
- And last, the appeal part of the message - what the speaker wants the listener to do.

For example...

A couple is standing in their shared living room. The one who works out of the home says: "Wow, the living room is a mess."

With this statement, there are four levels that this message can be interpreted on.

Sender: "Wow, the living room is a mess."

Factual Information: The living room is very untidy.

Appeal layer: Why is our house so untidy when you're here all day?

Relationship layer: You should clean it up.

Self-revealing layer: I don't like when the house is messy.

I want you to clean it before I get home.

Receiver:

Factual Information: The living room is very untidy.

Appeal layer: So, you're saying I shouldn't spend my time with the baby, I should leave her by herself in her crib and clean the house instead?

Relationship layer: You think my parenting is questionable.

Self-revealing layer: You don't understand the importance of what I'm doing spending time caring for the baby all day and *not* cleaning.

Because of the perceived intention of the message, the receiver might answer:

Receiver: "Sarah needs me to take care of her, not clean up the living room. If you want it tidy why don't you clean it yourself?"

What we need to take away from this four-ear model of communication is that it is very important to be clear when we are communicating. All the levels of our message need to work in harmony. If you are making an appeal, don't couch it in language that will make it difficult for others to understand that you are asking something of them. State it clearly and upfront.

As a listener, it's important to understand that what we hear is often not what the speaker intended to communicate. It is very easy to misunderstand and we should check back and restate what we think we've understood to make sure that that is what the other person intended to communicate.

As communicators, if we understand that it is very easy to misunderstand someone, then we will be more careful when we speak to be sure we are conveying what we want to communicate. And when we listen, we will be aware of the fact that it is highly likely that we are misunderstanding what we are hearing. We will use check backs to ask if what we heard was what the person meant. In that way, we will be more successful in communicating what we really wanted to say.

5 Axioms of Communication

This model is important because even though some of it is self-evident, these are the sorts of reminders that we need to think about when we want to improve our communication skills. The model was developed by the psychologist and communications theorist Paul Watzlawick. Having a good understanding of what people are really saying when they talk will help you understand what's going on in every conversation you have, so instead of mistakenly assuming that you know what the person is really trying to say when you don't, you will now know how to respond properly in each situation.

The five axioms of communication according to Paul Watzlawick are as follows:

1. You cannot *not* communicate.
2. Every communication has a content and a relationship aspect.
3. The nature of a relationship is dependent on the partners' communication procedures.
4. Human communication involves both digital and analog modalities.
5. Inter-human communication procedures are either symmetric or complementary.
6.

So, what in the world does that mean? Well, let's unpack each axiom to understand what exactly each one is telling us.

You cannot *not* communicate. This is referring to the fact that in any exchange, whether verbal or otherwise, you are always communicating. It's simply impossible to not communicate. Even if you do nothing, that is sending a certain message.

Every communication has a content and a relationship aspect. This is similar to the four-ears theory in that it's pointing out that in every exchange there is the content that is being conveyed and then there is another level that is what the speaker feels about the listener and what the listener feels about the speaker. For instance, if in the past you were the sort of person who made small talk without really caring about the other person, then your words would have been saying one thing, but your non-verbal communication would have been sending a very different message.

The nature of a relationship is dependent on the partners' communication procedures. This refers to the process of turning messages into meaning. It points to the misunderstandings that we talked about with the four-ears theory and comes back to the fact that just because you think you've conveyed your message clearly, it doesn't mean that the other person has understood it in the way that you wanted them to.

Human communication involves both digital and analog modalities. Digital just means *what* you say. Analog is *how* you say it. This is extremely important because if you angrily shout "I love you!", it doesn't exactly convey love. And the person that you shouted it at, probably wouldn't believe that you really loved them. When there is a discrepancy between the words and the tone/body language, people consistently believe the non-verbal language.

Inter-human communication procedures are either symmetric or complementary. Symmetric relationships are ones in which both parties are equal. Complementary relationships are unequal, where one of the people has more power than the other, for instance, in a teacher-child relationship.

So, in summary, whenever you have any kind of interaction, you are always communicating. There's always more than one level to the communication — there's the actual message and then there are other layers, such as relational aspects and non-verbal language. And in any human exchange, the interaction is either between equals or it isn't. These axioms are self-evident but sometimes you need to face the obvious and think about it.

Knowing about these models of communication will help you to be more aware of what's really happening in the conversation underneath the words. This, in turn, may help you diagnose what might be going wrong and the reason for it so that you can respond or change what you are saying accordingly, in order to improve the conversation.

Paying attention to the *way* that people communicate will help you to be a better communicator yourself. And, in turn, it will allow you to be great at small talk.

Non-Verbal Communication

Non-verbal communication encompasses any communication that is not words. So, it can include eye contact, facial expressions, the tone of voice — including volume and pitch, personal space, touch, gestures, posture, and appearance, as well as many other non-verbal cues.

More than half of communication is non-verbal, so it is very important that your facial expression, posture, and tone of voice all align with the message you're trying to communicate. Otherwise, you'll be misunderstood.

Maybe you want to be seen as an interesting person at a party, but you have a slouched posture, poor eye contact, a bored expression, and speak in a monotone voice. It is highly unlikely that anyone will find you interesting.

Non-verbal communication is more important than the words you say, so let's look at what your body is conveying. We will be looking specifically at facial expression, the tone of voice, posture, and gestures.

Facial expression

The expression on your face — in conjunction with your tone of voice — says more than the words that are coming out of your mouth. Of course, this is important in any exchange we have with another person, but it is particularly crucial in small talk situations because we are not talking about anything of consequence and so those non-verbal cues tend to convey more than our words. Sometimes someone may not be paying much attention at all to the words you are saying but is either enthralled or completely turned off by the *way* you are saying them.

Beneficial expressions that you might consider using would be the following: smiling, an open, interested look, a neutral yet friendly face, or twinkling eyes - this is where you smile with your eyes but don't really move your mouth into a smiling shape. Counter-productive expressions would include the following: a frown, a bored face, a scared expression, a nervous, agitated look in your eyes, or other expressions that convey negative emotions.

Tone of voice

The tone of voice is one of the most obvious ways we convey a meaning that's deeper than the words. And this will come through even if you are on the phone and can't see the person you are speaking to. Our tone can show how we are feeling and what we really think, even if our words say otherwise.

This is the reason why, when you ask how your friend is and they say that they're okay, you ask them if they're sure. Because the tone of voice they used when they said that they were okay was a clear signal to you that things were not okay at all.

We do this all the time. A family member tells us about their new job and we know that something is wrong, even though the words imply that everything is fine. And this works for good things too. Sometimes a friend only has to say hello and you may ask what they're so happy about.

Knowing this, you can take it into your small talk conversations as well. Some strangers that you talk to will be upset about something. If you notice that this is the case, you can ask them if they're okay, if they need help, or if anything is wrong. Most people won't overshare so if they don't want to talk about it because it's too personal, then they won't. But if it's a small upset, then they may tell you about it and that will get the conversation going as well as any other conversation starters.

Posture and gestures

Posture shows a lot about what you are feeling. A slumped posture tends to convey sadness, discontent, and giving up. An upright, alert posture might show happiness. If you have a lot of tension in your posture it might mean that you're angry if your chest is shoved forward, or fearful if your torso is caving in on itself.

And there are much more subtle aspects to posture that we

pick up on without knowing. Depending on the situation you're going into, you will want to choose a posture that makes sense. In a small talk situation, you are likely to want to come across as open and friendly, and so making sure you are standing up straight and lifting your head will convey that to the person that you're talking to.

Gestures and the movements we make when we speak can affect our message in different ways. Psychologists Wallace Friesen and Paul Ekman found six ways that non-verbal communication directly affects our speech.

We can use non-verbal signals to emphasize, to repeat, as a substitute for words, to regulate speech, and sometimes even to contradict what we are saying. Let's look at this in more detail.

When we use non-verbal cues to emphasize what we are saying, we might slam a fist down on the table or clap our hands or nod our head decisively. If we want to use gestures to repeat, that is when we will say no and then shake our heads. Using gestures as a substitute for words occurs when we actually don't say anything, such as nodding instead of saying yes.

When we use non-verbal cues to regulate speech, that means we pick up on the fact that the other person wants a turn to talk. For instance, when we finish up what we are saying and our conversational partner opens their eyes wider and takes a breath to speak, that is an indication that they want to talk. If we are paying attention, then we don't jump in with another comment of our own; instead, we allow them to tell us something. Most people do this unconsciously and we don't even realize what we're doing because these are the sorts of social skills that you pick up on as a child when learning to speak.

Sometimes the non-verbal message can contradict what the words are saying. An example of this is in a movie where someone has been kidnapped, the kidnap victim might have to say and look like everything is fine when she is talking to someone who is worried about her, but many non-verbal cues would be conveying that she's not fine.

Another example from the film of this contradiction would be when two men are speaking to each other and the conversation appears to be about something mundane, but there is a subtext in which one man is warning the other to watch out.

And lastly, the non-verbal cues often complement what we are saying. If we are feeling sad, we naturally slump so that others more easily pick up on the fact that we are unhappy.

How to Use Body Language When Making Small Talk

One of the best ways to make sure your body language is aligned with your verbal language is to set a clear intention before you enter whatever social situation you're going into. For instance, before you go into the meeting, the interview, the party, the lunchroom, take five seconds and create an intention for what you want to communicate. For the meeting, it could be power. For the interview, confidence. Maybe when you're going into a party or the lunch room, you'd like to convey friendliness or kindness or openness. Taking a few seconds to think about this will delegate it to your unconscious mind and allow that intention to shine through the words your speaking and into your non-verbal language.

SOFTEN for positive non-verbal behaviours

To remember positive body language there is an acronym: SOFTEN. The SOFTEN technique reminds you of what positive non-verbal behaviors to use during a conversation and was developed by Don Gabor in 2006. It stands for smile, open posture, forward lean, touch by shaking hands, eye contact, and nod. Using these sorts of non-verbal behaviors will encourage others to approach you.

Smile

This is obvious, but you will be surprised what you will forget when you are feeling ill at ease. People display all sorts of strange behaviors when they are uncomfortable in their surroundings. You don't want to make this mistake.

When you smile you show that you are friendly and not a threat. You will make others feel comfortable and indicate that you are open to conversing.

Open posture

Sometimes we use defensive, protective, or closed off body language and we don't even realize it. It happens when we are feeling uncomfortable and alone. Some of the most common postures are the following — your body on an angle, arms crossed, or hands in pockets. You don't want to put your body on an angle, which is a classic defensive position in martial arts. And you don't want to cross your arms over your chest, because this indicates you are protecting yourself. Hands in the pockets indicate that you're closed off, holding yourself close, and not interested in interacting.

Instead of these, you want to use an open posture, facing someone head-on with your arms at your sides. You'll also want to relax your jaw, neck, and shoulders. Even if you think you're looking chilled out, just do a quick body check and see if you're holding on to tension and if you are, let it go. Also, where are your arms? What direction are you facing? We are often so unconscious of our own body that we don't notice that we're going into defensive and closed off postures without even realizing it.

So, make sure you do a quick check every little while during a social situation. You just want to make sure you're still keeping an open and relaxed posture so that you're not turning away conversational partners before you even get a chance to open your mouth.

Forward Lean

When you're listening and speaking, a slight forward lean towards someone shows that you are paying attention to them. Be careful not to be weird with this one. It's easy to overdo it if you're just doing it because someone told you to and not because you actually feel it.

The reason these sets of rules exist is that someone watched what actual successful conversationalists were doing and made a list of their behaviors. If you just try to do what's on the list, it's going to come off as inauthentic. But if you're really paying attention and interested in what they're saying, then leaning in is a natural reaction and that's what you're aiming for.

Touch by shaking hands

A good firm handshake will show that you are strong and believe in yourself.

Eye contact

There are cultures where eye contact is avoided, but not in ours. If you want people to feel that you're listening to them, or if you want to make an impression on the person you're talking to, then maintaining proper eye contact is absolutely necessary.

That doesn't mean that you stare the person down. But keep a normal amount of eye contact while you speak with them. If you have difficulty either staring too much or you feel uncomfortable looking someone in the eyes for that long, you can try this tip.

When you are looking someone in the face during a conversation, move your eyes briefly between their forehead, cheeks, nose, chin, eyes, and mouth. The eye movements when you do this are so minute that the other person will not notice that you are not looking them in the eye the entire time. But because you are moving your eyes around all the time, you won't stare and you will not be looking them in the eyes the whole time and so you should feel more comfortable.

Eye contact implies attention and this brings us back to the first rule of communicating. Pay attention. And you can show you're paying attention by maintaining eye contact.

Nod

Nodding shows someone that you understand and are paying attention to what they're saying.

Exhibiting positive body language is extremely important when going into social situations and SOFTEN can give you a quick check to make sure you are presenting yourself in the best light possible so that people will want to come and talk to you.

Part 2

Small Talk Apprentice

I f you have not had much success making small talk in the past or you have done it but it has been a nerve-wracking experience for you, then preparing to make small talk will be necessary. You will need some mental practice. And if you have an understanding friend or family member, you may want to try out your efforts on them. Only practice with someone who is understanding because you don't want your efforts undermined by someone who doesn't get what you're trying to do.

Why is it important to have the proper mindset when going into a social situation? Well, it has to do with your inner state. If you are negative and upset, those sorts of feelings communicate themselves to the other person through your body language, facial expression, tone of voice, etc. If you are feeling good and confident, that is also conveyed through your behavior and words. So, it is very important to work on your inner state before going into any social situation. This sort of inner work may make the difference between you making successful small talk or having a terrible time where, in conversation after conversation, you crash and burn. Before you read this book, you may have blamed your failure on the other people, the host, the mood at the gathering, or the weather. But now you will know that nearly every negative thing that happened was because of the choices that you made.

Are you starting to see how having a good mindset is crucial to being successful at small talk?

Create a Positive Mindset

Mindset is a huge area of personal improvement and entire books have been written on the subject. Mindset is basically the framework that all your thoughts take place in. For instance, if you have a growth mindset then when you run into an obstacle or difficulty, you are more likely to believe you can overcome it, to try different solutions, to persevere when things are hard.

Whereas if you have a mindset that says... I can't do anything... then you will be much more likely to give up when a challenge arises. You are more likely to believe that there isn't a solution to the problem. And that it's impossible for me to do things like that. Now, none of that is true, but your mind makes it true. Just like it will make your positive mindset true as well. In this book, we will just get into the aspects of mindset that can positively or negatively affect your ability to make small talk.

First of all, why is a mindset so powerful? Mindset is what tends to give your unconscious mind direction. So, if you have a negative mindset, then all the power of your unconscious mind is being directed to creating negative situations, whereas if you can maintain a positive mindset then your unconscious mind will be helping to create positive things in your life.

Mindset is a bit like the architectural plans for a house. When the carpenters begin, they review the plans. But when they are actually in the middle of building the house, they are focused on the one part, say the kitchen cabinets, that they are making right then. But in the background, they have a bigger picture of how the entire house needs to look when it's done and that is there in the background as they work on the smaller details.

Similarly, you need to have a blueprint for how you want your social interactions to go and that is your mindset. When you consider your overall mindset, then when you're in the midst of a specific conversation, of course, you're paying attention to what's happening at that moment, but in the background, you have that global idea of how you want your social interactions to go in general.

Having a positive mindset will affect both the words that you speak as well as your non-verbal language, in order to bring about the kind of positive social experience that you want. It will make you more willing to try new things that you've never done before. And it will help you persevere when your plans don't go the way you hoped they would. Now let's have a look at aspects of your mindset that will affect your ability to make small talk.

Trust in your own value

This is actually a hard one for many people. Although we often say that we value ourselves, when we get into social situations, the truth comes out. We behave in ways that show others that we *don't* value ourselves and then, in turn, they find it difficult to value us — even if they want to.

So, to begin with, you must believe that you have something interesting to say. What if you don't? Well, that is beyond the scope of this book and there have been many books written on developing self-esteem and belief in yourself that you can read.

But for now, here is an exercise that might help. Sit by yourself and ask yourself the following question. *What is wrong at this moment?* Not two days ago when you burned the soup, or in five minutes when you're going to forget to put on the washing. But right now. If you're being truthful, there's probably nothing wrong at this moment. Your mind likes to tell yourself that you suck. But that's just your mind being negative.

Sure, we all make mistakes. But that doesn't mean that we ourselves are *wrong*. When you bring it down to this very moment that you're in right now, you'll probably find that there's nothing much wrong right now, which could help you to see there's nothing wrong *with you* right now either.

Whatever you do to accomplish this, the second big key to being successful at mastering small talk — after giving true attention to the other person — is to actually feel that you have value to add to the world. Think specifically about a strength, or something you really enjoy doing and are probably good at. Or maybe you can remember times in your life when you felt confident and happy - like a fun trip you took. These are all things that you can likely talk about and will be interesting to people who don't know you. You can have particular topics or stories in mind that might be fun to discuss, so if your mind goes blank about what to say in a social situation, you can call up these ideas and have something ready-made to talk about.

Be kind to yourself

Being kind to yourself is very closely linked to feeling your own value. You need to shut down your mind when it starts being cruel and telling you that you are terrible in social situations, that you should just give up, and that no one is ever going to want to talk to such a loser. Your mind can be more unkind to you than your enemy ever would. So, it's important to have the right attitude towards yourself if things go wrong during a small talk conversation. If you've said something stupid or inappropriate, there's no point in getting angry with yourself. Instead, try to look at the funny side of what happened. Probably the person you were talking to didn't even notice. We are all more preoccupied with ourselves and whether we are saying the right thing to take much interest in mistakes other people are making. Staying positive is important so that you don't start getting mad at yourself, which can create a downward spiral. And you don't want that. Things will not be perfect all the time. Sometimes people say silly things. It happens. Get over it, shake it off, and move on.

Stop fearing being judged

This one is difficult because the terrible thing is that other people do judge you. It's the way people are. The mean part of the mind that is cruel to yourself also likes to make itself feel better by being judgemental towards others.

So, it's not a matter of never doing anything that others could judge you about. That's impossible. Even if you lay in your bed and never moved or spoke, people would find something to judge you about. "Why doesn't that person get up and do something?"

There is absolutely no way to prevent other people from judging you. The trick is not to worry about the fact that they're judging you.

Now, again, this is difficult because most of us have been raised to worry about what other people think. Comb your hair, you look like a hobo. Stand up straight, only losers slouch. We have a lot of parent's, teacher's, and other people's voices in our heads telling us to definitely worry about what other people think.

The good news is that this is simply a habitual thinking pattern that you have got into and that you can get out of. People tend to have similar fears and doubts; everyone is worried about being judged by others. Remembering this can make you feel better about approaching someone to talk to them because you know that they are probably as nervous as you are. If it seems clear that they are nervous too, you can even make that a shared experience to start the conversation.

Another way to avoid the fear of being judged is to genuinely care about the other person you're speaking to. If you are focused on them and on making them feel comfortable and being kind to them and interested in them, then it is easier to ignore your mind telling you that everyone is looking at you and judging you.

Feel you are part of the group already

This is a visualization technique that you can use before you go into a situation. Take a few seconds and see yourself as part of the group, see yourself smiling and talking easily. This will prime your mindset with positivity and give you a powerful expectation for the good that is going to come out of the upcoming encounter.

Whatever your mind believes, it tends to make come true. So, giving it a positive image to work from will make it more likely that you will have a positive outcome from whatever situation you find yourself in.

You can visualize for a couple of minutes in the morning before you get out of bed, or you can even just stop for a few seconds before going through the door into the office where you're about to have a meeting with your boss. It doesn't have to take long, just use the power of your mind for good, instead of letting negative imaginings dictate the end result of your interactions.

By creating a positive mindset, you will prepare yourself for having a good conversation, a good day, and, in the end, a good life.

General Rules for Small Talk

It goes without saying that these rules are good guidelines for conversation and... well, life. So, bringing them into your life in a much more holistic way than just your small talk practice is a good idea.

Listen

There is nothing people want more than to be listened to. Every person wants to be seen, recognized, and listened to. So, listening, as half of the small talk equation, is one of the best gifts you can give to the person you are talking to.

But listening does not just mean being quiet while the other person speaks. Sometimes people think that's all that listening is. And in the meantime, while they wait for the other person to finish talking, they are thinking about what they're going to say. Or even worse, sometimes they're thinking about something else entirely.

True listening, though, is something entirely different. You need to be quiet inside, really paying attention to the other person. Listen to the words, but also pay attention to the other cues you are getting that pertain to the message that the person is actually trying to convey.

This kind of listening requires you to be quiet and still inside, instead of thinking about what you want to say. You look into the person's eyes. You hear the words. You observe the other cues you're getting.

Then when it's your turn to speak, you have absorbed the message that the person wanted to give you. And you can respond in a way that shows that you have been listening and paying attention. You can make an insightful comment. You can ask a good question. You can respond with a story of your own that shows that you were listening to the other person and that you understand.

If you start listening in this way, you may notice that your conversational partners are *not* practicing true listening. But there's no need to be offended. Not everyone can listen in such a deep way. You, as a small talk master, will be able to practice this kind of listening.

Be curious

This is sort of an obvious one but most people don't practice this conversational rule. It seems as though we are so caught up in our own stories that we forget that everyone else has a story too. And maybe there are some people who truly are not interesting in the least. But if you really listen and pay attention to another person, you will likely find something interesting about them.

The reason we often don't find others interesting is that we are so enamored with our own story that we simply don't care about anyone else's. Or, we are glossing over the person and not really seeing them at all and that makes them seem boring to our minds.

If you listen and pay attention truly, you will find that people are far more fascinating than you ever gave them credit for. Everyone has a story. And if you start to learn about someone else's story, you will begin to discover untold secrets and treasures that you never knew were there.

Try looking at each person that you make small talk with as a treasure chest just waiting to be opened and the jewels within revealed. Imagine how curious you would be if you had found a treasure chest and were about to open it. You can bring that same level of curiosity to every person you meet.

Provide information about yourself

Clearly, when you speak to someone you will likely tell them something about yourself or your life. Or maybe you're the sort of person who doesn't say anything about themselves when they talk to someone they don't know well. This could be the reason that you haven't been very good at small talk in the past.

As mentioned above, it is good to listen with your whole attention focused on what the other person is telling you. But then when they stop speaking, you may find that a thought comes to you that you want to share. And you share it. You may tell a story that relates to what they just said. You may comment on how you dealt with a similar situation that they just told you about. This is true conversation and will allow you to make a real connection with the person, no matter how brief your exchange.

The difficulty lies in knowing how much about yourself you need to share. In general, a good rule of thumb is to let the other person say more about themselves than you say about yourself. The last thing you want to do is be that person that blabs on and on about themselves and never lets the other person get a word in edgewise.

But neither do you want to be the person who seems cold and distant because they refuse to share even the smallest detail about themselves with the person they are talking with.

You will not become a small talk master, nor will the other person feel heard, just because you are silent and let them do all the talking. It requires you to actively participate in the conversation and show that you have heard and understand what they have been telling you.

It is necessary to strike a balance between listening to the other person and sharing small details about yourself or your life experience. Generally, you should err on the side of caution and let them do more talking than you do, while at the same time not letting the conversation lag.

Be respectful

This is pretty obvious but sometimes, when people are nervous, they'll make jokes or comments that are maybe not respectful, simply because they are not thinking straight. You must avoid doing this. Clearly, no one is going to want to keep talking to someone who is rude, so make sure you keep your jokes and comments about others respectful. If you are feeling nervous or anxious, it's important to focus on the other person and ask them about themselves, not say things that others may consider offensive or disrespectful to themselves or others.

Be honest

People often play roles when they go into social situations. They play the role of the successful business person, or the supermom, or the charming gentleman — or sometimes we play a negative role, like the irresponsible person.

But usually, this is not what others are looking for in their interactions with you. What they really want is someone who is real. If you are talking about yourself, be honest if you have had difficulty with a certain situation, no matter how trivial. Don't pretend to have it all together. This tends to turn other people off and can even come across as bragging.

If they mention a situation that's been bugging them, listen to it and respond appropriately. Maybe the bus they take to work is always late or the weather's been rainy lately. It's annoying to have someone tell you that their bus is never late or they would never even *take* the bus. Or that the sun always shines on their side of the city.

Instead, sharing a similar experience, even if it isn't recent, would be more appropriate. For instance, maybe you tell the story of when you were a kid you used to hate when the bus was late and you would have to walk into school when everyone else was in class because you felt like you had done something wrong.

The person may enjoy your story as an amusing anecdote but they will also feel heard on a deeper level because you are showing them that you really get why it annoys them when the bus is late.

These sorts of conversations are what will turn you into a small talk master, a good conversationalist, and the kind of person that people will want to talk to again.

Watch non-verbal cues

When you are speaking with someone, remember from Part 1 that there will be levels to the conversation — even if it's only small talk. The person you're talking to may tell you that they've started a new job with a smile. But then they may sigh and drop their eyes.

This is a non-verbal invitation to ask them what exactly about their job isn't going the way they thought it would. The person's body language seems to be indicating that something isn't quite right. So, you could begin by asking them how it's going. They may say that it's going well but there's an aspect of it that they didn't anticipate, or that they feel they're not good at or that sort of thing. This gives you a chance to respond in a way that shows that you've heard and understood them.

Most of the time, though, your small talk conversations won't be about such important matters. Whether it's an important topic or a trivial one, you still need to watch the other person's body language.

Maybe you're at a party and you ask the person you're talking to how they know the host. When the person answers, there is a tightness to their voice and their face has shut down. This is a non-verbal cue that the person has some issue with the host and perhaps it would be best to move on to other more safer topics.

If you ignore those sorts of cues, you could go on yapping about how much you like the host and how great the party is and you would be completely alienating the person you're talking to. This is not what a small talk master does.

It all goes back to the number one rule: pay attention. If you're paying attention, you'll know which topics are subjects you should continue and which ones aren't.

Detect clues

This section continues on from the previous one, in that once you have picked up on the person's body language, then you know what to do in each small talk conversation. Sometimes you may choose to continue the conversation if the person seems to be enjoying it.

If you start getting the feeling that they're bored based on their body language, then maybe you want to ask them something about themselves. People usually enjoy telling others about their life and that may stave off a dangerous conversational lag.

On the other hand, if you feel that the person really does not want to talk to you, it is better to move on. There is no shame in moving on if the conversation is not going well. You can excuse yourself to use the restroom, get a drink, or go do something else that will allow you to make a graceful exit from the conversation.

The truth is that it is simply easier to connect with some people than with others. If the first person you are speaking with is not a good fit, make a graceful exit from the conversation and try again with someone else. Just because the first conversation didn't go as well as you had hoped, does not mean that you have done something wrong. It just means that maybe you need to find a more similar person to have a conversation with.

Although, as for that, you can never tell by looking who you may connect with. It is simply a matter of talking to the people who you get a chance to talk to, pay attention, and see what happens.

Be emphatic

Nobody likes a so-called *yes man*, who is always agreeing with everything the other person says. Nor do people enjoy talking to someone who has no opinion on anything. When you're talking to someone, feel free to express your opinion without being overbearing. It is not necessary that the other person *shares* your opinion. But you can voice it respectfully and see what they think about it. This leads us directly into the next rule.

You don't have to be right

A conversation is not an argument. Not everyone has this problem, but for the people who do it is a really serious issue. Some go into a conversation with their sword drawn and their knife between their teeth, ready for a fight. If you are one of those people, you must remind yourself before you attempt to make small talk with someone, that not everyone has to think what you think.

It is okay to disagree. If someone says that the new paint job in the lunchroom looks great, you don't need to pounce on them if you don't think so. You can just nod in a way that shows that you heard their opinion. A nod doesn't always mean that you absolutely agree with what the person said, so it's not being dishonest. You can also state your opinion with a fairly neutral statement, such as, "I think it might have looked better in blue."

This implies that you don't particularly like the pink they used, but it also doesn't body-slam your conversational partner and give them the feeling that you are fighting with them. Maybe your colleague will point out that colors have an effect on mood and perhaps they didn't use blue because it might have lowered workers' energy in the afternoon, following lunch.

Because you didn't jump on the other person and smite them with your opinion, which is, of course, the correct opinion, your comment might instead be the opening into a truly interesting discussion about the effects of colour on mood and energy, which you would never have had the chance to have if you had been aggressive in your conversational tactics.

First Impressions

Don't judge a book by its cover. This is a great saying, except, um, that's exactly what everyone does. If a book doesn't have a good cover, it doesn't matter how great the story is; nobody is going to take a second look. It's the same thing with a first impression.

People are social creatures. We have evolved over the millennia to connect with others. And we assess a person in the first moment of looking at them and in the first minute or so of talking to them.

This doesn't give you much time to make a good first impression. You need to consider your appearance — clean, tidy, and appropriate clothing for the situation you're in — because if you don't, you may not get a chance to practice your small talk skills on anyone.

Once your general cleanliness and proper attire are established, the next thing you want to think about is the body language you're using as you enter the situation.

Are your shoulders hunched and your eyes down, indicating that you're nervous or afraid? Are you frowning and sending *keep away* vibes? Or are your shoulders back, your arms relaxed at your sides, a pleasant or neutral expression on your face?

You need to remember what we learned in Part 2. We are always communicating something before we even say a word.

Make sure you're communicating what you want to and not your default old habits.

If you have a habit of slouching, then make an effort to stand up straight when you're entering a social situation. If you tend to frown, you'll want to deliberately relax your face. This is because people will read your body language as you approach and if you're sending the wrong message, they will not even want to start a conversation. They won't even give you a chance to say anything.

There are three main things to think about both before and as you enter a small talk situation. First of all, presence or the way you establish yourself in the conversation. Second, positivity and third, that all-important eye contact.

Presence

Everyone always says that you need to have a presence in a social situation. People with a presence get noticed, have people waiting to talk to them, and seem at ease no matter who they're talking to. It is that indefinable something that makes charismatic people charismatic. You may think that those people have something you don't, but this isn't so. Anyone can have presence. Read on to find out how to develop your own presence.

The beginning of developing your own true presence is avoiding taking on a persona or trying to act like someone you're not.   You need to be rooted in yourself and communicate that to others. If you can do this, you will give off an authentic and true presence that others will be attracted to.

But how?   Well, presence starts with being rooted in yourself and feeling your own presence. You can do this by trying this short exercise. Sit by yourself and hold your hand up in front of you. Keep it still and close your eyes. Now, without moving your hand or opening your eyes, ask yourself...

How do I know that my hand is still there?

If you get quiet and still, you will be able to sense your hand. Once you practice a bit, you'll be able to sense your whole body, even with your eyes open. That is your own presence. Then when you go into a small talk situation, you can feel your presence and when you're well-grounded in yourself that way, others will pick up on that.

Another way you communicate presence is by really paying close attention to the other person. If you watch a charismatic person in a conversation, you will notice that they seem to be really interested in what the other person is saying. This is not an act. They really are interested. That's part of what makes them such a presence in the room. They aren't acting a part, they are being authentically themselves. And that is such a rare thing that people are startled and captivated by it.

Before you enter a small talk situation, take one breath and feel your presence. Then go into the conversation ready to be interested in the other person. You will be surprised at the difference in the quality of the small talk you are able to make.

Positivity

Be positive. That's what you hear so much these days. But what does it mean? And how can you be positive when you are anxious about a social situation or meeting new people?

You may not be able to completely get rid of your nerves, but there are some things you can do to have a more positive mindset when entering a small talk conversation.

You can begin with a quick visualization before you go into the social situation. See it playing out positively. See yourself having a presence in the room, paying attention and really being interested in the people you're talking to, and generally enjoying yourself during each conversation you have.

At first, this may seem fake or silly. That's okay. Do it anyway. You can imagine it in your mind like a movie. Some people don't actually see it happening but only speak the words in their mind.

Remember when we talked about mindset and that, whatever your mind believes, it makes true? Well, this is where we use the power of the mind to create the kind of situations we want. Obviously, you can't control every detail and it won't necessarily turn out exactly the way you visualize. But using this technique will definitely improve your social situations. Will every one be perfect? Probably not. Will they all generally improve? You will most likely be pleasantly surprised.

Why does this work?

The reason visualization is such a powerful technique is because your mind can't tell the difference between you imagining something and it actually happening. If you wanted to improve your free throws in basketball, you could practice in your mind and you would actually improve your accuracy more than if you practiced physically.

Why? Because the same neural pathways are activated when you visualize... but there are no mistakes!

Practice doesn't make perfect. Perfect practice makes perfect. And this is how you can practice something perfectly. It works for free throws or playing the piano. And it can work for small talk, too.

You can also use a positive word or phrase to keep your mind focused on positivity. Now, you would not do this when you're in a conversation because then you wouldn't be paying attention to the person. But you could use it as you enter and leave or when you're not speaking to anyone.

Simply keep repeating a word or a phrase, such as, thank you, people are cool, or I am great at small talk. If any phrase feels false, then don't use it because it would defeat the purpose. 'Thank you' is a simple positive thought that will keep your mind focused and not let negative talk creep in. It is a good one to use if you can't think of anything else.

Part of the problem with a person's presence in a small talk conversation is the mental chatter that's going on in their minds around the conversation. If you can keep this mental noise to a minimum, it will help you pay better attention to the other person and have a stronger presence in the situation.

Eye contact

We have discussed eye contact in a fair amount of detail before, but it is so important in making a good first impression that we will look at it once more in light of how to use it to establish a good rapport with the person you're talking to.

To begin with, let's look at some eye contact fails. What are some of the things people do that send the wrong message?

You don't make eye contact at all. You not only don't make eye contact but you look at your phone instead of at the person. You stare in an intimidating way. You make eye contact but then slide your eyes away in a shifty manner. You blink excessively. You keep looking away at other people and things.

These all send the message to the person you want to talk to that you either don't care about them at all, or they shouldn't trust you, or you have the attention of a goldfish and aren't worth wasting their time on.

None of these is the message you want to convey, but that is what your eye contact is telling them. You may actually really want to talk to the person but they will not know that, based on the eye contact body language that you are using.

So, what is really going on? You may find making eye contact uncomfortable for many reasons, but if you want to be a small talk master, you have to be able to do it. Let's examine each behavior and see if we can determine what's causing it and what to do about it.

You don't make eye contact at all.

What could be happening:

You find eye contact so uncomfortable that you don't want to do it at all. Or maybe you find the person intimidating. Maybe they are superior at work or an attractive person of the opposite sex that you would like to approach.

What to do about it:

1. Get over it. Feel your own presence and just look them in the eye.

2. Too hard? This may be the case for people who experience social anxiety. Okay, well then look near their eyes. If you focus on their eyebrow or just under their eye, it will still seem as though

you are looking right at them but may lessen the anxiety you feel.

3. Practice getting better and more comfortable with this essential social skill. If you have someone close to you that you can practice with — a friend or family member — try making direct eye contact for varying lengths of time. Eventually, you should feel better about making eye contact with strangers or people you don't know very well.

You not only don't make eye contact, but you look at your phone instead of at the person.

What could be happening:

Same as above but you're using your phone to distract you from the discomfort you feel.

What to do about it:

Stop! You're being rude. It doesn't matter what everybody is doing. Being on a device in the presence of another person in a social situation is simply rude. You need to stop doing it. If you need to check your phone, go to the bathroom or the lobby and do it discreetly — when you're alone.

You stare in an intimidating way.

What could be happening:

A lot of people, when they feel intimidated by a situation or a person, will not shrink into themselves but will actually puff up and try to dominate the conversation in an aggressive way, since this seems to lessen their uncomfortable feelings. But this is no way to become a small talk master. People who are really good at small talk, never make their conversational partner feel intimidated.

What to do about it:

Before you go into a conversation, sense your presence. This should lessen your need to have to be in charge of the conversation a little. Then, when you feel the urge to stare someone down and be aggressive, take a breath and *don't*. Instead, soften your gaze and ask the person about themselves. This will take the pressure off you and hopefully, you will start to feel better about the conversation, which will mean that you don't feel like trying to dominate anymore.

You make eye contact but then slide your eyes away in a shifty manner.

What could be happening:

You're making an attempt at eye contact but once you feel the person's gaze on you, it makes you uncomfortable and you move your eyes away. Of course, this sort of avoiding eye contact will definitely give the other person the wrong idea about you. Everyone's seen the movie with the man (or woman) with the shifty eyes. You don't want to trust him (or her). And you don't want to go near them, never mind have a conversation.

What to do about it:

This is the same issue as the first one we discussed where you don't make eye contact at all and it has the same solution. Either just get over it and hold eye contact even though you find it uncomfortable, focus near the eye without looking directly at them, or you could also practice with someone you trust to become more comfortable making eye contact.

You keep looking away at other people and things.

What could be happening:

1. You don't find the person interesting, you're bored, and don't want to be talking to them. By the way, whether this is true or not, that *is* what you are communicating.

2. Or maybe you do find your conversational partner interesting but you find other things in the area *more* interesting.

3. You could also be having the same issue as old shifty eyes above, where you are uncomfortable holding eye contact, but you move your eyes

59

away from the other person's in a normal sort of way.

4. Or perhaps you have focus issues where your brain itself is having difficulty concentrating on the conversation even though you want to.

What to do about it:

1. What if the person is really not interesting to you? And you really do wish you'd chosen someone else to speak to? If this happens, it's important to remember to be respectful of the other person. And also keep in mind that just because you don't find them interesting, doesn't mean that they actually *aren't interesting*. That's just your opinion, at that particular moment in time.

What you can do is to continue the conversation, paying proper attention and not letting your eyes or mind wander, until it comes to a natural ending point and you can excuse yourself.

*But what do you do if the conversation does not come to an end because you are talking to someone who likes to create a conversational black hole, which other people get sucked into and never come out again? This will be dealt with at the end of the book in the

Troubleshooting section.

2. What if you find the other person interesting but there are other *more* interesting things because maybe you are at an exciting party or conference? If this is the case, it's simply a matter of being disciplined. Tell yourself that you will get to the other interesting people and things later. Right now, you are talking to this person and that is what is the most important and interesting thing. Zero in and pay true attention to the person and what they are saying. The next moment when you are with those other people or things that *seem* more interesting is actually not going to be any better than this one. Be patient and really listen to the person you're talking to, the way you want to be listened to by others when you're talking to them.

3. If you are having trouble making eye contact or holding eye contact, it is a skill that you have to develop. See the first eye contact problem, above.

4. If you have actual focusing issues, then you likely deal with this challenge in all parts of your life. Solutions to this are beyond the scope of

this book. But you may already have strategies that help you focus and you can apply them to help you focus when making small talk as well.

Nerves and Social Anxiety

What if you are too nervous to even contemplate talking to a stranger? Here are three techniques you can use to calm yourself before you enter a social situation or conversation. You can also use them while in a conversation if the anxiety comes up again, though you will also need to pay attention to the other person at the same time.

How can breathing help?

Breathing deeply stimulates the vagus nerve, which in turn activates the parasympathetic nervous system in the body. This system is responsible for calming you down by slowing your heart rate and breathing and relaxing your muscles.

We can harness the calming power of the parasympathetic nervous system by using breathing techniques to bring down our anxiety levels. The following two techniques use breathing to help you calm yourself.

Technique #1: Am I still breathing?

Ask yourself the question... *Am I still breathing?* Then check by taking a conscious breath. Pull the air in through your nose and pay attention as it travels all the way down into your abdomen. You should feel your belly move out a little as the bottom of your lungs fills up with air. Taking even just three conscious breaths in this way will bring immediate relief from nerves and anxiety.

Technique #2: Counting Breaths

This second breathing technique brings the power of breathing together with focusing the mind in order to both bring in the positive and keep out the negative. Pull the air in through your nose and pay attention as it travels all the way down into your abdomen. You should feel your belly move out a little as the bottom of your lungs fills up with air. This will bring a calming feeling to your body. But what about when your mind starts up again, telling you how bad this party, or meeting, or conference, or wait at the bus stop is going to go?

That's what the second part of the technique is for. Once you have taken a couple of conscious breaths, then pay attention to your breathing while counting each breath — or alternatively, you can count each in-breath and out-breath. Count to ten and then start over. We do this so that your mind can't put it on autopilot and then keep thinking in the background.

By focusing your mind on counting, you keep it busy, which prevents it from thinking negative thoughts about yourself, the situation, and other people. Often our nerves come from all the bad scenarios our mind is imagining, so keeping ourselves from imagining them in the first place is incredibly useful.

Technique #3: Focus on the Senses

Another way to keep your mind busy and not think negative thoughts is to pay attention to sense perceptions. You can go through each sense and pay attention to one thing you notice from each. Use your eyes, ears, nose, sense of touch, and possibly taste if you're eating or drinking.

For example, I enter a party and immediately notice that it is decorated in green and yellow (sight), there is the smell of cinnamon from the cider that is being served (smell), I hear the clinking of dishes in the kitchen (sound), I brush a piece of lint off my pants and feel the smoothness of the fabric (touch), and then I go to the bar and get a drink; its taste is sweet and fizzy (taste).

While you are paying attention to all these sense perceptions, your mind has no time to feel nervous. So, when you are approached or approach someone with your drink in hand, your nerves should be a lot calmer than if you hadn't used the technique.

Try practicing these methods at home and then they will become second nature when you are out in social situations. If you find it too distracting, then don't use them during a conversation, but only before and after. These techniques can also help you relax after a stressful day or fall asleep more easily.

Part 3

Small Talk Master

Now we are getting to the good stuff. In this section, we will get into the details of making small talk. Who you should talk to, how to get started, some techniques you can use to help you know what to talk about, how to keep it going, and how to end a conversation. We'll also discuss some difficulties you may run into and how to handle them. This section is going to give you all the tools and techniques that you need to become a small talk master.

First Rule of Conversation: Complete Attention

The first and most basic rule of communication is to give your complete attention to the person you're listening to. Make eye contact. This is so essential because in Western culture it is the most important way to show someone that you're listening to them. Look at the person and not at anything else. Then, make sure you're listening with your mind to what they are saying, not just preparing your next remark. And finally, respond in a way that shows you have heard what they said. This sort of listening and paying attention makes the other person feel that you care about what they are saying.

And whether you are talking to your partner or someone you're standing next to in line, the thing that people want most is to be listened to. Not just tolerated. So, give someone your complete attention when you are interacting with them. What else do you have to be doing anyway? You're talking to this person right now. So, just listen to them. Talk to them. Give them your focus and attention. They will appreciate it. And you will be making your first step towards being proficient at making small talk.

Some behaviors that definitely need to be avoided when engaging in small talk with someone are the following: Avoid looking at other things or other people when the person is speaking. And definitely avoid checking your phone. When you're not looking at the person that you are speaking with, it gives the impression that you don't care about what they are saying. Even if you do care, have been listening, and can recite back verbatim what they have just said, they will think that you don't, based on your body language.

Other people can sense when you are not really paying attention to what they are saying. And if you have had difficulty with small talk in the past, it was maybe because you just didn't care about what the person was saying and that showed. If you would like to truly master the art of small talk, then you are going to have to change your way of thinking about other people.

Every single interaction you have in a day has value. Every single person you meet, even if it's for the smallest of interactions, has the potential to either add value and good to the world or to simply be yet another transaction without connection between two people. You will decide which sort of interaction it will be, based on how much true attention you give to the people that you meet.

Who To Talk To

Some situations put you in a spot where you don't have a choice of who you talk to. For instance, when you are seated next to someone at a table, there is no choice in who to make small talk with. It's the person sitting next to you. No need to make a choice. Just start talking.

But when you are in a social situation and you need to choose who to talk to it can be quite a nerve-wracking experience. Having to choose a small talk conversational partner can happen at a party, a conference or workshop, a networking event, a wine and cheese, a bridal or baby shower, in a doctor's or dentist's waiting room, etc. All of these circumstances require you to approach someone you don't know and have a conversation. In a waiting room, you might not always have to speak to the person, but sometimes people will speak to you. So, the person you choose to sit beside may become a conversational partner.

Group versus One-on-One

You will need to make your choice based on what is going on with you at the moment. Sometimes you may feel braver and more confident than at other times. It is important to recognize how you're feeling at the moment and whether or not you can handle the social situation you're putting yourself in. There is the question of whether to approach one person standing by themselves or try to join a group. There are pros and cons for each choice, which we will look at in more detail in the following section.

Approaching a person standing alone

Here are some of the pros of joining someone standing by themselves. It is less intimidating than approaching more people at once — going up to one person can seem a lot less daunting than going up to five people already in the middle of a conversation.

Also, the person standing by themselves may be as nervous as you are and they will be grateful that you were brave enough to come up to them — bonus points for earning good karma, plus you now have something in common to talk about.

And when you actually have to speak and say something, you are only saying it to one person and so that is less worrying too.

But there are some cons to approaching one person by themselves. What if they are actually standing by themselves for a good reason? They want to tell you about their bunions or they're a conversational black hole that will never stop talking and you'll never get away. This is possible. But the probability of this actually happening is low. And in the Graceful Exit section, we will give you ways of getting out of a conversation that never ends.

What if the conversation freezes and there's only the two of you to restart it and neither of you seems up to the task? This is also a possibility, but you have your conversation starters to get things going again. Or you can make a graceful exit and get out of there.

So, there is a good side and a bad side to going up to a person who is standing alone, but generally, it's less intimidating than approaching a group and that has to do with how our brains are wired.

Approaching a group

Here are some of the pros of approaching a group of people instead of a lone person. First of all, it's easier to sneak up and join in without drawing too much attention to yourself. Then when you feel comfortable or have something to say, you can insert yourself into the conversation without as much stress or feeling that you have to carry it.

You can sometimes start a side conversation connected to the main conversation with a person who is close to you. So, in a way you use the group as a bit of a shield until you're feeling confident enough to speak to someone one-on-one.

If you've assessed yourself and determined that you simply don't have the energy or presence to engage in small talk at the moment, then a group may the perfect solution. Not having social energy to engage can happen with an introvert who is extremely depleted, or someone with social anxiety, or anyone who is physically not feeling well. Joining a group of people can allow you to be a part of the social environment without feeling inadequate or having to use energy that you don't have in interacting with others.

So, the pros look pretty appealing. But the cons of approaching a group can be pretty nasty, so you have to choose wisely. Approaching a group that is mostly composed of strangers who are speaking to each other will likely be a success because they are all outsiders and don't mind another joining them. But if you happen to approach a group of people who all know each other it can mean bad news for you and your fragile, budding small talk skills. If you go up to a group where everyone knows each other, you will likely get puzzled looks or frowns, or even eye rolls that indicate you've trespassed where even small talk masters fear to tread — a clique.

These people are all talking together and consider themselves an entity. And they do not take kindly to strangers just waltzing up to their circle and interfering.

This is a sort of social maiming and you may not come out of it without scars. We don't want this to happen. So, be careful when approaching groups because the pros are worth it if you make good choices.

One of the ways you can assure yourself of being accepted by the group is if someone introduces you. Maybe you're at a networking event and an acquaintance of yours can introduce you to the group. This will allow you entry into a group in which everyone already knows each other because you have been vetted by someone they know.

Another way to avoid this social maiming is to assure yourself that the group doesn't know each other. You may be able to ascertain this by various clues that you've picked up throughout the event. If you're sure, then go ahead and join them.

For the brave soul, you can also walk into a group that knows each other and simply introduce yourself and then use a conversation starter, like FORD perhaps, which we will be discussing next.

Make a decision based on each individual situation

It's up to you to make your choice based on how you are feeling. Are you confident and peppy or tired and suffering from low energy? You should also pay attention to the vibe of the crowd at the event. Are the people seeming open and friendly? Or snobby and clique-ish? And lastly, you need to gauge the individual person or group that you wish to approach. Are they sending keep away signals? Or do they seem approachable? Only you can make the decision. Some will work out well and some may not. But the only way you will get good at this is by trying, so give it a go.

Conversation Starters

When you start a conversation, it's important not to sound too contrived. Some websites will give you conversation starters or ice breakers that are frankly ridiculous, and if you use them to start a conversation, you will definitely get some weird looks.

Shared Experience

One of the easiest ways to start a conversation and one that makes the most sense is to comment on, or ask a question about, something that you are currently both experiencing.

For instance, if you are at a wedding reception, you could make a comment or ask a question about the ceremony itself that you and the other person have both just attended and now have in common.

If you are waiting at a bus stop, you could remark to the person you're standing next to about the weather, or whether the bus is on time or late.

Here is another example in a work/professional situation. Maybe you are at an industry conference and you are at the Meet and Greet and talking to someone that just happened to be standing next to you.

Being at the conference is something you have in common, so you could start with that. You could ask if the person flew in for the conference and whether they have decided which break out session they want to attend.

Some conversationalist *specialists* will tell you that mundane things, such as the weather, are not interesting enough. But a shared experience is something that you *already* have in common with this stranger you're trying to talk to. And what brings people together is having something in common.

If you are in the same place as someone, you have something in common in that you are currently having a shared experience. You are both in that moment in that space together. Maybe you're at a party, or waiting in line, or at an event. Wherever it is, you are there together and there is always *something* you can comment on.

Also, you can use an interest you have in an article of clothing they're wearing as a starter as well, because that is something you have in common. If you really like their coat or some other thing that they're wearing, then you can start off that way.

"That's a nice coat! What company makes it?" Then a conversation about how warm it is, whether it has enough pockets, or what sort of material it's made of can ensue. This is an easy opener that both the person starting the conversation and the other person can feel comfortable with because it is right there in front of you both, and this makes it easy to ask questions about it. And it is a shared experience in that you are both interested in it.

This is the easiest beginning there is — to talk about a shared experience. Then you can move on to using the FORD or ARE techniques, which will be discussed in more detail later on in the book. Or maybe the person will make a comment about something you are curious about and then you can ask them about that and the conversation will ensue.

Ask what you've been wondering

Often you will see someone that you want to talk to and part of the reason that you want to talk to them is because you find something about them fascinating.

Wow, that woman's hair is really shiny. I wonder what sort of shampoo she uses?

That guy is so charismatic. I wonder what he does for a living? Professional speaker, maybe?

The dark brooding guy in the corner is so hot. I wonder why he's not talking to anyone. Does he have a fascinating secret?

Being brave and bold and going and simply asking

someone a question about themselves that you've been wondering, or making some comment about them is a good way to start a conversation in a more interesting way, but still being natural and authentic.

For instance, with the first comment, you could go up to the woman and say, "Your hair is beautiful, what shampoo do you use?" This may lead her to tell you and maybe she gives you some other hair tip like she washes it in goat's milk or something too. Of course, this would lead you to ask where she learned to milk a goat. Just kidding. But the conversation will probably naturally flow from there. When things are winding down and you are ready to move on, you can thank her for telling you about the shampoo and mention that you're going to check it out.

With the charismatic guy, you could go up to him and say something like the following: "I've been watching you for the past couple minutes and you seem so comfortable chatting with people, I was wondering if you're maybe a public speaker?"

Maybe the man laughs and says, "Nah, I'm a plumber. I'm just good with people." This can lead you to ask about his job. Who does he work for? What sort of jobs does he do? Or you could say that he seems as though he'd be really good as a public speaker from what you can see. There are quite a few different ways the conversation could go. But starting with a question, which also doubles as a compliment can be a good start — as long as you mean it and aren't just trying to be smarmy and schmooze people.

And as for the brooding man in the corner, you could go up to him and say, "I saw you standing here looking all dark and brooding and I wondered if you have a fascinating secret."

Now, you have to be the sort of person who can ask a question like this naturally. Many people couldn't. But if you can, it might start an interesting conversation. It could turn out that he tells you that he's just nervous about starting to talk to someone because he's not very good at small talk. Ah, shared experience! You can say that you are a little nervous too and ta-da, the conversation has begun.

Ice Breaker Comments

Well, here are some ice breaker comments if you really want your conversations to be exciting... and you're not worried about getting weird looks from some people who aren't used to such interesting talk.

"If you could only eat one food for the next five years, what would you eat?"

"If you won an all-expenses-paid trip, what place would you go to?"

"If someone paid you $100 000 to eat a bowl of beetles, would you do it?"

"What is your hidden talent?"

"If you had a superpower, what would it be?"

If you're brave/crazy enough to use these ice breakers, you may end up having some of the most interesting conversations of your life. Of course, some people may just think you're crazy and walk away. But, nothing ventured, nothing gained. If you're feeling confident, give it a try. The worst that can happen is you find out who the uptight people are in the room.

Often the hardest part of small talk is getting started. And once you have begun, it's just a matter of being truly interested in the person and asking questions about them. Then you share some things about yourself when it's appropriate. And voila. You have made small talk.

Small Talk Techniques

There is a myriad of techniques that you can use to make small talk if you have not had much success with it in the past. But we are not going to talk about every single method you could use. That would be confusing and unnecessary. There are two techniques that are tried and true that will be presented in this section. People have been using them for millennia to talk to other people that they don't know well.

Since the beginning of time, people have been asking other people about these same topics. But some kind people have put them into a memory-friendly mnemonic device so that when we're under pressure we can still remember what we can talk about with the stranger in front of us.

In the following chapters, we will talk about the ARE, FORD, and SOFTEN techniques to help you remember the small talk basics and become relaxed and natural when making conversation.

The ARE technique

In terms of all the techniques that have been developed for making small talk, the ARE method seems to be the best for beginning a conversation. The method was developed by communications expert Dr. Carol Fleming in 2010. The method takes two strangers who know nothing about each other but who happen to be thrown together and it allows them to begin to get to know each other.

If a conversation is like a dance, then this method gives you the steps to begin. The acronym ARE stands for Anchor, Reveal, and Encourage.

The A in ARE stands for Anchor. An anchor is an object that holds another object in place. It keeps you in one spot, rooted. The Anchor is about being where and when you are and using it as a conversation starter to make small talk.

This is similar to what we talked about in the previous chapter about using shared experience to begin a conversation. It is the thing that makes the most sense because it is right in front of you. And it is something that you *already* have in common.

Some methods have you searching for somewhat arbitrary or kind of fake things that you could possibly have in common, or even making up things to have in common. But when you are with someone in the same place, you have something in common — the present moment of where and when you are. And there is always something to say about that. Even if you are in a bare room with no furniture, no decorations, and no one else, you can always comment on how bare the room is, how uncomfortable it is to sit on the floor, and how you got into this strange place to begin with.

Anchor

So, Anchoring is all about taking the first, perhaps tentative step towards a stronger connection with this person. It is all about using your surroundings as inspiration for beginning the dance. You could mention the place you're in, what the weather is like, or other people (respectfully, of course). If you're at an event/party you could make a comment about the food and drink, the entertainment, the venue, or the decorations. Or you could comment on something positive about the other person, such as what they're wearing or doing.

Conversation #1 - Anchor

You're at a workshop for teachers and the person beside you is trying to adjust her abnormally low chair before things get started. You comment, "Why are there so many levers on that chair? It seems like overkill."

She looks up and smiles.

"I have no idea. And I don't know which one to press to get it to go up."

"I think it's this one." You point to the one that you think makes it go up. She presses it and it goes up.

"Thanks," she says. "I'm Marlee."

And the conversation continues.

Conversation #2 - Anchor

You're waiting for the elevator with someone that you've seen around who lives in your building. You say, "This elevator always seems to take so long to get down here."

"Yeah," the person comments.

"Unless I'm coming in with an armload of groceries," you add with a smile. "Then it arrives and leaves again before I get anywhere close."

The other person laughs and says, "Yeah, it's slow. I should probably take the stairs but I'm too lazy."

"Me too," you say.

The conversation continues from there.

Conversation #3 - Anchor

You're at a party where you only know the host and he has abandoned you to greet new guests. You decide to approach an attractive guy that you'd like to talk to. He's at the snacks table and you join him.

"Wow, what a spread," you say, helping yourself to a plate and starting to choose different things to eat.

"It's pretty amazing," he says, giving you a smile. "Lot of fish."

"There do seem to be far too many fish dishes," you comment. "Maybe there was a sale on seafood."

He laughs at your little joke and you feel a little burst of confidence. Maybe you can do this small talk thing after all.

In each of the three conversational examples, the person starting the conversation Anchors themselves and the person they're talking to by commenting on a current, shared experience.

Reveal

The next letter in the ARE acronym is R for Reveal. This part of the method is about revealing a bit about yourself in relation to the Anchor you just used. This is done in order to strengthen the connection between you and the stranger or acquaintance that you're talking to. When you open up even a tiny bit it's showing the other person that you want to connect with them.

This is where you can add your opinion (not controversial) about something. Or comment on something in a way that shows a bit of your personality and who you are. And it also gives them something to talk about that will allow you to extend the conversation. You dance a few steps towards the person to see if they'd like to dance a few steps back at you. Let's look at where the three examples would go next if the person used the Reveal part of the ARE method.

Conversation #1 - Reveal

"Why are there so many levers on that chair? It seems like overkill."

"I have no idea. And I don't know which one to press to get it to go up."

"I think it's this one."

"Thanks," she says. "I'm Marlee."

"Nice to meet you, Marlee," you say, extending your hand. "I'm Emma and I teach Grade Four."

Conversation #2 - Reveal

"This elevator always seems to take so long to get down here."

"Yeah."

"Unless I'm coming in with an armload of groceries," you add with a smile. "Then it arrives and leaves again before I get anywhere close."

"Yeah, it's slow. I should probably take the stairs but I'm too lazy."

"Me too," you say. "Besides I do enough stairs at work."

"Oh yeah?" the person says, showing interest. "Where do you work?"

"At the Clark Building on 7th street," you say. "Three floors. No elevator. I'm the one running the files up and down between partners on different floors."

"So, you're a lawyer?"

You nod. "I'm trying to make partner, which is why I'm the one running the stairs."

Conversation #3 - Reveal

"Wow, what a spread," you say, helping yourself to a plate and starting to choose different things to eat.

"It's pretty amazing," he says, giving you a smile. "Lot of fish."

"There do seem to be far too many fish dishes," you comment. "Maybe there was a sale on seafood."

He laughs and you feel a little more confident, enough to share a little more about yourself.

"Wow, what a spread," you say, helping yourself to a plate and starting to choose different things to eat.

"It's pretty amazing," he says, giving you a smile. "Lot of fish."

"There do seem to be far too many fish dishes," you comment wrinkling your nose a little. "I must say, I don't understand the appeal,"

"You don't like fish?" he says.

You shake your head.

"Me neither," he says. "But I am appreciating the fifteen

different kinds of cheese."

"Ah, now that's a food I can get behind," you say with a smile. "I do love me some cheese."

In each of the examples, the person went on to share something about themselves and gave the person a comment to respond to in order to continue the conversation.

In Example #1, she shared her name and what she teaches. This is very simple and straightforward. She keeps it light. She's not baring her soul, just giving some basic information about herself.

The guy in Example #2 makes the comment about doing enough stairs at work which piques the other person's interest and gets the other person to ask where he works. Then he reveals that he's a lawyer in the Clark Building and that he's trying to make partner. This is a fair amount of information but it also explains the stairs comment and that makes it reasonable.

Example #3 has the person giving her opinion on the food, particularly about the fish. She throws the first comment out there lightly and the guy could have ignored it if he actually liked fish. But because he doesn't like fish either, he latched on to it as a shared experience that they can then talk about. They then both share that they do like cheese, which opens up a new area of discussion.

All of these conversations begin with the Anchor — their shared experience of the present moment. And then continue on because the conversationalist shared something about themselves. Nothing too crazy, just a tiny opening. If the person you are speaking to wants to continue talking, they will take the opening. If the other person ignores the little opening then that probably means they don't want to talk to you and you should move on. But for the right person who does want to talk to you, that opening is their first glimmer of the person that you are and if they find it interesting, then they will gladly continue talking in order to find out more about you.

Encourage

The last letter in the acronym is E for Encourage. This part is all about following up on the tenuous connection you've established. But it's also about allowing them a chance to dance a few steps themselves. So far, since you initiated the conversation, you've been doing most of the heavy lifting. At this point, you need to give them a chance to talk, to respond, to share their thoughts.

If they don't seem to be making any attempt to continue, then based on that and their non-verbal cues, you'll probably take that as a sign that they don't want to talk to you and end the conversation. But if they do answer in a way that continues what you're talking about and their body language communicates that they are interested in you, then you know that you've found someone to talk with for the next few minutes and a connection has been successfully made.

Conversation #1 - Encourage

"Why are there so many levers on that chair? It seems like overkill."

"I have no idea. And I don't know which one to press to get it to go up."

"I think it's this one."

"Thanks," she says. "I'm Marlee."

"Nice to meet you, Marlee," you say, extending your hand. "I'm Emma and I teach Grade Four."

"I teach Grade Four too," she says. "What school do you teach at?"

"Riverside."

"Oh really? I worked there my first year of teaching."

Conversational goal accomplished — meet other teachers so that I don't feel awkward and uncomfortable in this setting where I don't know anyone.

Conversation #2 - Encourage

"This elevator always seems to take so long to get down here."

"Yeah."

"Unless I'm coming in with an armload of groceries," you add with a smile. "Then it arrives and leaves again before I get anywhere close."

"Yeah, it's slow. I should probably take the stairs but I'm too lazy."

"Me too," you say. "Besides I do enough stairs at work."

"Oh yeah?" the person says, showing interest. "Where do you work?"

"At the Clark Building on 7th street," you say. "Three floors. No elevator. I'm the one running the files up and down between partners on different floors."

"So, you're a lawyer?"

You nod. "I'm trying to make partner, which is why I'm the one running the stairs."

The elevator opens and you both get in.

"So, what do you do for a living?" you ask, since the conversation has begun to center on you and you know that people don't enjoy conversations with a speaker who talks only about themselves.

"I'm a personal trainer," the person says.

You smile.

"Well, I guess you get enough exercise at work, too, then."

The person laughs and gets off at their floor.

"See you around," you say.

"Yeah, see you."

Conversational goal accomplished — make interesting conversation with a stranger while waiting for and riding on the elevator so that I don't feel uncomfortable with the silence.

Conversation #3 - Encourage

"Wow, what a spread," you say, helping yourself to a plate and starting to choose different things to eat.

"It's pretty amazing," he says, giving you a smile. "Lot of fish."

"There do seem to be far too many fish dishes," you comment wrinkling your nose a little. "I must say, I don't understand the appeal."

"You don't like fish?" he says.

You shake your head.

"Me neither," he says. "But I am appreciating the fifteen different kinds of cheese."

"Ah, now that's a food I can get behind. I do love me some cheese. What's your favorite?"

"Definitely Brie, but I really enjoy Monterey Jack on grilled cheese."

"That sounds amazing."

"Yeah?" he says, his eyes lighting up. "Maybe I could make it for you sometime."

"That would be great," you say.

Conversational goal accomplished — meet a cute, interesting new guy at the party and see where it takes us.

In each example, the ARE method allowed the person to easily and naturally make conversation with someone they didn't know. The ARE method allows you to ease into speaking with someone in a way that doesn't make the other person feel like you're making uncomfortable small talk. It is a method that uses the way that real small talk masters make conversation, but breaks it down in a way that's easy to remember and gives us lay people a chance to develop the same small talk abilities.

The most valuable thing about it is that it seems to allow the conversation to flow in a natural way and doesn't seem as though you are using lines or doing anything fake to start speaking with someone.

Practice the ARE method as you make small talk in the next few days and see how it will help you to have easy conversations with people you don't know or that you only know slightly.

The FORD small talk method

This chapter begins with a caveat. Though the ARE method is very useful for beginning conversations, the FORD method is more appropriate once you are further into the conversation. I first heard of this approach to communication from "Practical Psychology". If you open with the FORD method, you will probably come across as nosy or too abrupt and inept socially.

The FORD acronym stands for Family, Occupation, Recreation, and Dreams. And, as you might imagine, these are not exactly *starting a conversation* material. These topics can be full of landmines and can cause the conversation to blow up in your face.

What if you ask about the person's family and they are recently divorced and lost their children, or their mother just died, or they're an orphan. You simply cannot just dive into these topics. Instead, start with the ARE method. Get the conversation going. Then use conversational cues that invite you to use the FORD method to talk to the person about things that they have an interest in.

Although extremely obvious, the FORD method is also highly effective for the main reason that *this* is how you ask people about themselves, as we mentioned in the earlier sections. *This* is how you know what to ask about. The FORD method comprises all the best small talk questions wrapped up in one neat four letter package. *This* is what will make you a likable small talk master.

In this section, we will discuss each letter individually and give examples of questions you can ask about each category.

Family

I'm sure the FORD method starts with the F for family because everyone has one and this makes it a universally shared experience. Now, as mentioned above, you *could* end up asking someone about their family and be meeting an orphan or someone who's lost family and for whom the topic is painful, but there's a very small chance that that will happen.

And though it's unlikely that talking about family will not work out, there is a possibility, and so it's important that you should use conversational cues to determine when it's appropriate to ask someone about their family. If they give you a short answer and show by their body language that it's not a subject they're comfortable with, then you should move on to another topic. In general, though, you don't have to worry too much. Most people will be happy to talk about their family, making it a really good topic to move into once the conversation is started.

Occupation

This is another good one to use once you're into a

conversation. Most people have jobs, so it is a great subject to use to continue a small talk conversation that you have started. There are usually many things you can ask each other about your respective occupations.

If you have similar or the same careers, then you can get into the details. And if you have a different career than another person, then usually there's plenty of things you can ask them about it that you don't know. Sometimes you have partial knowledge about that occupation because someone you know has that job, so then you can ask them comparative questions based on what you know about the job and whether theirs is like or unlike that of the person that you know.

For instance, if you have a brother who's a chef you can ask questions based on what he's told you that his job is like. You can ask the chef in front of you whether their experience has been that it's a very stressful job with long hours and not the best pay. You can ask whether they like the sous-chefs that they work with. And if the waiting staff they have to work with drive them crazy or if they're competent and capable.

Recreation

This part of the acronym is meant to remind you to ask people about what they do when they're not at work. You can ask if they have a hobby or what they like to do in their free time. Once they tell you, there is usually a myriad of questions you can ask or comments you can make. Again, either you can get into the nuts and bolts if you have that pastime in common, or you can ask questions to learn about their hobby. Either way, conversational opportunities abound.

Dreams

Now, this one you have to be careful with because it can feel a little like prying, or seem weird if you don't use it properly. You for sure wouldn't open with Dreams.

"Hi, my name is Michaela and someday I'd like to be an astronaut. What is the dream that's dearest to *your* heart?"

Uh, yeah, no. That is not what a small talk master does.

Definitely not.

A person who is adept at small talk starts with ARE, with a shared experience, and then moves into FORD — asking about things that are more important to the person. Then, and only if the person seems open to it, you can talk about something like Dreams.

You also don't have to call it a dream, which seems a bit strange for a normal conversation you're having with an almost stranger. Instead, you could ask about their future plans or something that they've always wanted to do without seeming like a weirdo.

Honestly, this one really should be used for deepening the conversation once you have established a rapport and a connection with someone, which will be discussed in more detail in the Keep It Going chapter. When you're meeting someone for the first time, you definitely don't want to come off as someone who shares too much information or asks questions that are prying in the first few minutes of the conversation. Those people are the ones standing alone at parties for good reason. You don't want to be one of them. You are a small talk master. And you have excellent social skills. And you know how to ease into a conversation — you'll get to discussing their hopes and dreams later. Much later.

Other Acronyms

There are some other versions that use From for the F. And Motivation or Message for the M. We will discuss these briefly because they could be useful additions to your conversational toolbox.

From

Some versions of the FORD method use From as the F. This is actually much better than Family as a conversation starter. Asking someone where they're from, especially if you're at a party or conference, is an appropriate conversation starter. It's light enough that most people won't have a problem talking about it. It's not going to make anyone uncomfortable.

And if you're at a conference, people will have arrived from different places, so it makes sense as something to ask about.

But it's also fine in regular life as a generic sort of question to ask someone, whether they're from the city or if they just moved there. It is a good one for strangers to talk about because of it being one of the most non-touchy subjects you can bring up. It's very neutral territory for strangers to begin talking about.

Motivation

Motivation is similar to Dreams in that it is finding out what is truly important to the person and should be introduced late in the conversation with a person. There are some acquaintances with whom you would never discuss such things. You really need to pay attention to the person and decide whether this would be an appropriate topic of conversation for you to pursue. In most small talk situations, it's not going to be.

Message

This tends to be a closure in a networking situation. You end the conversation with a message that you want to connect again and you exchange contact information or set up a time when you'd like to get in touch again.

You would not use this in a social situation. It's a way of

ending a work conversation where you're either hoping to work with the person or you would like them to be your client. In the case of them wanting to hire you, you would give them your card or write down your info. And maybe you would set a time when you would get in contact with them again. A message is all about leaving the person with a clear sort of directive for what you'd like them to do next, in terms of working together.

Example conversation using the FORD method

Let's look again at one of the conversations from the ARE method chapter, where two teachers meet at a workshop. Notice how the person starting the conversation begins with the ARE method and then gravitates to the FORD method. Which method is being used is indicated in square brackets throughout the conversation.

[Anchor — talking about a shared experience, adjusting the chairs at the workshop]

"Why are there so many levers on that chair? It seems like overkill."

"I have no idea. And I don't know which one to press to get it to go up."

"I think it's this one."

"Thanks," she says. "I'm Marlee."

"Nice to meet you, Marlee," you say, extending your hand. "I'm Emma and I teach Grade Four."

[Reveal — the R from the ARE method, she shares her name and occupation]

"I teach Grade Four too," she says.

[Occupation — the other person is using the O from FORD, talking about their shared career, which is teaching]

She goes on and asks, "What school do you teach at?"

[Encourage — the E from the ARE method, she asks a question to draw you into the conversation]

"Riverside," you answer.

"Oh really? I worked there my first year of teaching."

"Cool. What did you teach?" you say.

[Encourage — the E from the ARE method, you ask another question to keep the conversation going]

"Well, my first year I had to teach anything I could get, so I took the temporary music position."

"You did? Do you play an instrument?" you say, interested.

"Yep, piano and guitar."

"Really? My son is taking piano lessons," you tell her.

[Family — this is the F from FORD, you share that you have a son]

"That's great. My daughters are learning the violin and it's hard for me to help them. It's so different from piano."

[Family — this is the F from FORD, she shares that she has daughters]

"Do you still play?"

[Recreation — this is the R from FORD, the conversation moves a little away from family to what the two women like to do in their spare time]

She tilts her head back and forth.

"Not as much as I'd like to, I spend so much time on work and with my son that it doesn't leave much time for hobbies. I basically try to get to a yoga class once a week and call it quits."

"I get it. My main hobby these days is a cup of tea and a good book. I probably should do something more active but I just don't have much energy. Like you say, after work and the kids, there's not much left for me."

"Yeah, I get you. It's a hard act to balance."

You nod.

***

A little later in the bar at the hotel, you meet the woman again and get to talking. After a few drinks and some more in-depth conversation, you return to her comment from earlier.

"Remember how you said that it's a hard act to balance?" you say. She nods and takes another sip of her drink.

"Well, I sometimes wish I could chuck the whole teaching thing and become a bestselling author."

"Really?" she says, her eyes wide. "That would be awesome. Like J. K. Rowling."

"Yes, I'd love to sit in my office and not have to deal with crazy kids. All I'd have to deal with were crazy characters."

"Sounds like you'd be living the dream," she comments.

"Exactly," you answer.

How to keep the conversation going

Some people are fine with starting a conversation but after the first comment ends in a one-word answer and the one after that ends in a one-word answer, they give up or don't know what to do.

There are a few things that could be going on here. First, the person you're talking to could be no good at small talk, too. If that is the case, it is important to use the FORD and ARE methods to help draw them out and get them talking about themselves so that they will forget their awkwardness.

Second, the person could, possibly, not find you interesting. Ugh. Doesn't feel good to be on the receiving end of that, does it? Try to remember this when you think that some are *not interesting*. It's really such a disrespectful thought to not think that a person has anything about themselves that you might find interesting. And when the person you're talking to clearly doesn't find *you* interesting, it feels pretty bad to be on the other end of that attitude. Of course, if this happens, either they will excuse themselves or you can excuse yourself, because there is no use talking to someone who is not interested in talking to you.

Open-ended Questions

The other problem could be with the way you're trying to make small talk. There are some questions that really don't require more than a one-word answer. Often adults direct these sorts of questions at children.

How was school?
How old are you?
My how you've grown!

Of course, the last isn't even a question. But you can see how those sorts of questions don't lead to conversation. And then the adult wonders why the child has nothing to say and supposedly won't talk to them. Instead, it's important to ask open-ended questions.

What sorts of things did you do in school today?
Who is your favorite book/TV show character?
You're getting so big, what kinds of things do you get to do now that you're getting older?

These are examples of both one-word answer questions, which discourage conversation and open-ended questions that invite a more complex and complete reply. Obviously, you want to use the open-ended questions, which will lead to conversation, instead of to silence. This is the most important thing that you have to do to keep a conversation flowing.

Provide information about yourself

Now that you are getting some small talk practice asking questions, make sure *you're* not the person answering in one-word responses. If the other person is asking you open-ended questions, then usually it's easy to give a longer answer. But even if someone asks you questions that require only a one-word answer, you can still elaborate and give more than the question is asking for.

Here is an example of an open-ended question and answer.

The other person asks you, "So, how are you liking the conference so far?"

Possible answer: "It's great." Or "Not so much."

But as a small talk master, you, of course, do not give such short answers. You would say something like, "Oh, it's great. I really enjoyed the keynote speaker. I got some useful takeaways that I'm going to put into practice right away on Monday."

This may inspire the other person to ask you what you found interesting and you can tell them. Then they'll tell you what they found useful and instantly you are having a conversation.

But you may have a person who is not as good at small talk

and they ask you a question like, "Did you enjoy the keynote speaker?"

Which could be answered with a simple yes or no. But you are a small talk master, so you will not give such a curtailed response. Instead, you can say. "I *did*. I thought the presentation was great. I took about three pages of notes. What did you think?"

Then the person will either agree with you or disagree. Either way, you have something to talk about. Just don't get into an argument. That's not small talk. Please see the section on dealing with different opinions in the Troubleshooting section if you are the sort of person who is likely to start arguing during a conversation.

If appropriate, deepen the conversation

Now sometimes small talk gives you a chance to make a genuine connection that leads to friendship. If this is the case with you and the person you're talking to, you may find it appropriate to deepen the conversation by talking about subjects that are closer to your heart or a little more private.

This may not happen in the first few minutes of the conversation you have with the person. But at some point, you may want to talk in more depth about things that you have in common that are a little heavier than the light sort of conversation that small talk usually calls for.

This is fine as long as you are both on the same page. This requires you to read the non-verbal cues and the content of the words that the other person is saying as well. If you misjudge, the person will be giving you signals that you have communicated too much information. It's weird when someone you don't know well overshares something personal, right? That's because it breaks social rules. So, make sure that you both seem to be connecting at the same level.

But if you are sure that the other person is interested in taking the conversation to the next level, then conversing is very enjoyable and could lead to a long-term friendship.

An example of how this may happen might be that you begin the conversation talking about your work as a teacher, but then somehow you end up on the subject of how you wish you could change the system to better serve what kids really need.

Or perhaps you have been chatting about your families and the other woman tells you that she is having a hard time with her oldest son being away at university. You are also finding it hard, so you start sharing how difficult it is for you too.

Maybe you have a shared experience with something difficult, like being bullied, fighting in a war in the military, losing your job, or getting divorced. The experience that you share doesn't always need to be positive.

Two people often bond more over unhappy experiences because the other person understands your pain. It's easy for anyone to say that they get it when you tell them you like going on walks because you find them invigorating. But most people are not going to be able to understand when you tell them that your business went bankrupt. Only certain special people will get what you went through when that happened. And when you find someone who understands difficult things that you've been through, it can be a real chance to make a friend.

Again, this is assuming that you are both enjoying the light conversation and are ready to move on to deeper topics. In general, you probably should avoid touchy subjects until you're sure the other person is ready for a deep conversation. But if you meet someone at a two or three-day event, then you may get to know them well enough that you want to talk about more important subjects that are closer to your heart.

How to exit a conversation

Most people are usually concerned about starting a conversation. But once the talking has petered out, one of the most difficult things is exiting the conversation gracefully. There is nothing worse than the awkward silence when both people have run out of things to say and don't know how to move on.

Read on to find out how to have a graceful exit to each conversation you have. The first thing is figuring out the timing of the conversation. A conversation is a bit of a dance between two people. As previously mentioned, you need to pay close attention to the other person, watch for non-verbal cues, and allow the last chance for the other person to add any final comments. If all this has been done and the conversation seems to be over, then it's time to move on to your closing statements.

One of the trickiest things is timing. You need to pay attention to what's going on in the conversation. Watch for when it's reaching its natural end, then you need to see if the other person has anything else to say and if they don't, then move into closing statements.

Closing statements usually finish up your chat with expressions that convey that you've enjoyed speaking with them. "It was great talking to you." Sometimes they imply or overtly state that you'd like to speak with them again. "Hope we can chat again sometime." Often, they'll include a goodbye in them such as, "See you later." Or "See you around."

Read on for some examples of different closing statements you can use in different situations. Once you've practiced chatting for a while, these will feel natural and you won't have to think about them.

Closing Statements

There are a few different ways of closing a conversation and you can choose the right one for the right situation. If you want, you can role play with your trusted friend or family member in order to practice different parts of your small talk conversation, so that when you actually get into the real situation it will flow fairly smoothly.

Closing #1 - Nice to meet you.

If you have just met the person, you can end the conversation by saying, "So, it was nice to meet you." Or "It was good meeting you. I hope we'll have a chance to chat again." Or "I'm just going to go get another... drink/etc. It was good talking to you."

Closing #2 - I have to use the restroom.

You can always say you need to use the restroom and excuse yourself, especially if the conversation isn't going well. "Will you excuse me, I need to use the restroom? It was nice talking with you."

Closing #3 - Well wishes.

If you know what they're doing next you can wish them well with what they're doing, such as, "Enjoy the breakout session. We can compare notes later and tell each other what we've learned." Or "Have a good time at your next meeting. I hope the performance evaluation goes well." Or if you've discussed an upcoming event, you can give them well wishes for that. "I hope your daughter's dance recital goes well."

Closing #4 - See you.

If you've been chatting with an acquaintance, you can simply close with, "See you." Or "See you around." Or "Have a good morning/day/afternoon/evening." Or "It was nice to see you." If it's around the holidays, you can say, "Merry Christmas." "Happy holidays." Or for another holiday that you know they celebrate, you can wish them a happy that — whatever it is.

Closing #5 - Interrupting the Conversation

Sometimes you have to cut the person short because something really has come up. Or at other times you may have been sucked into a conversational black hole from which no one ever escapes. (See the chapter on Troubleshooting for more on this.) If either situation happens to you, you may need to interrupt the person.

The important thing is to not make the person feel as though you are abandoning the conversation because you aren't enjoying it. Even if you haven't been enjoying it, there's no need to make another person feel bad about that. Sometimes there's just no connection and there is nothing wrong with leaving, as long as you do it kindly and respectfully.

If you have to actually interrupt what they're saying, you could say, "Excuse me. I'm so sorry to interrupt, but there's been an emergency at home and I have to go."

You would only say this if there really is an emergency or whatever it is that's interrupting the conversation. Because there is nothing worse than making up excuses to get out of talking to someone like they do on some TV shows. In real life, that won't fly because eventually that sort of selfish behavior will come back to you and you will regret your actions.

Remember what was discussed at the beginning of the book. Respect the other person. Pay attention. Be present with them. Then if you have to go, do it with respect once again. Tell the truth. And if you need to leave because you simply haven't connected with that person, saying that you need to go to the restroom is correct because you do just need to go there and collect your thoughts and be ready to try again with someone else. There's nothing wrong with this as long as you use kindness, honesty, and respect.

If you don't have to actually interrupt them but there is a pause in the conversation, then you can interject your closing. "I'm sorry to have to cut our conversation short, but I've got to go. I'm helping set up for the next speaker. It was so nice talking to you, though."

Closing #6 - Take care/Have a good...

If you are not going to see them again for a long time or maybe you will never see them again, you can say, "Take care." This is a universal expression that implies that you wish them well and that they take good care of themselves till you meet again. It would be appropriate if you've been at a conference with the same people for a couple of days and you've got to know them, and now you're leaving and will probably never see them again. Or maybe not until next year's conference.

You can also use specific good wishes here such as, "Have a good flight/drive." Or if they've told you about something coming up, you can comment on that. "Good luck with that presentation to your boss." Or "Good luck with the guy at the coffee shop. You should definitely ask him out." Or maybe if you've got into some deeper conversation with the person you could say, "Good luck talking with your son about him moving out. I hope it goes well."

Exiting a conversation gracefully takes some practice but you will get better at it the more you practice your small talk skills. The main thing is to convey that you've enjoyed talking to the person and that you hope to talk to them again. Naturally, you would only say that you hope to speak to them again if you really mean it.

If you don't want to talk to them again, that's fine. Remember to be respectful. And you can use a simple closing that shows you've enjoyed speaking with them but doesn't really leave them with the sense that you are open to conversing again. Most people will pick up on this and will be fine with it. If you didn't sense a connection with them, then probably they didn't sense one with you. A lot of the time, it goes both ways. And there's no harm done in parting ways with respect and moving on to find someone that you resonate with and that you'll enjoy speaking to more.

If you are parting from someone you likely will not see again at all or not for a long time, it's appropriate to use comments that show that you've enjoyed talking to them.

Then wish them well in the future.

Example Conversations

In each conversation, there are explanations in the square brackets of what techniques and methods the people in the conversation are using to help you understand what's going on.

Example #1

You are a new teacher at a school and you have gone to the Wine and Cheese event that was organized. You are standing by yourself and notice another teacher standing by themselves. You decide to go talk to them. Since this is a work event, you have several easy starters. You could introduce yourself by saying your name and what you teach. No doubt the conversation will flow from there.

"Hi, I'm Miranda Novak and I teach grade nine and ten math."

[Anchor — your shared experience is both of your being teachers]

The other teacher smiles and shakes your hand.

"Hey, I'm Grace Darling. I teach grade eleven and twelve English."

"English? Wow. I'm impressed. I'm more of a numbers

person."

[Reveal — you tell something light about yourself, you're better at numbers than words]

"I like them both," Grace says. "I actually love teaching math too. But when I came here, English was the only position open, so I took it. But if I had a chance I might switch back."

[Reveal — this prompts her to reveal something about herself, she enjoys both numbers and words]

"Really," you say. "That's interesting. Usually, people are good at one or the other, not both."

Example #2

You are having some work done on your vehicle and the service station offers rides to work. Your workplace is a ten-minute ride away, so you are stuck in the vehicle with this stranger in silence for all that time.

There are a few starters that you could use in this situation. You could start by asking them if they have other tasks they do for their job, other than driving customers. You could ask if they like their job. You could ask whether they like working for that particular business.

If you don't feel comfortable asking about their job, you could start by commenting on the weather. Everyone has an opinion on the weather and it's something that everyone can either rejoice in or commiserate with, depending on what is happening on that day.

You could also comment on the traffic or lack thereof.

Sometimes a person who does this sort of job begins to make conversation first. If this is the case then you just have to make sure you are answering in complete sentences and asking them questions about themselves. The conversation will roll on naturally from there.

"I'm going to 364 Moore Street," you say to the man giving you the ride.

"Sure," he answers.

"Really mild winter we're having this year, don't you think?"

[Anchor — the mild winter is a shared experience and is a light topic of conversation]

"Yeah, I haven't even got my winter clothes out yet. I've been making do with my fall jacket," he says.

[Reveal — he is open to conversing and he tells something about himself, he hasn't got out his winter clothes yet]

"Oh wow. I have to have my hat, scarf, and mittens, even in fall. Or I'm freezing. You don't get cold?"

[Reveal — you tell him something else about yourself, you get cold easily] [Encourage — you ask a question, he doesn't get cold wearing such light clothing]

"Nah," he says with a laugh. "I'm hot blooded; my

ancestors were Scandinavian. We're good with cold."

[This gives you plenty of conversational paths that you could take from here. You could ask about his ancestors who came from Scandinavia and whether he still has family there. You could ask about how long he has lived in the city and if he ever has been to any of the Scandinavian countries. You could inquire further about his abilities to withstand the cold and at what temperature below freezing he would actually take out his winter coat. Etc.]

Example #3

You are walking your dog at the park and you see a pretty woman that you want to talk to sitting on a bench, but you're nervous. You use the Counting Your Breaths technique for a minute until you feel calmer . Then you go up to her and start a conversation using the ARE method to get things going.

"Hi," you say, pointing beside her. "Is this seat taken?

[Not the best opening, but it *is* a shared experience. And you *are* nervous.]

"No, go ahead," she says, gesturing to the open spot.

You sit down and have your dog lie down quietly beside you. The two of you sit in silence for a moment, then she comments, "That's a pretty quiet and well-behaved dog you have there."

[Reveal — she's giving her opinion on your pet]

You smile.

"He sure is. He's a rescue and I've had him since he was a puppy."

"Aw," she says, leaning over to look at the dog. You continue on because her body language indicates she's interested in what you have to say about your dog.

"He's happy as long as he's near me. He probably wouldn't be as content if I went to an office every day. But because I work from home, he doesn't have to be cooped up alone all day. Every day we come for a couple walks here."

"Really," she says. "What do you do?"

[Moving on to FORD. She has inquired about your occupation, which takes us to a further level of small talk. So far so good.]

"I'm a computer programmer," you tell her.

"Cool," she says, impressed.

"What do you do for a living?" you say to get her to talk more about herself since you realize that you've maybe been doing most of the talking.

"I'm a contemporary dancer in a dance troupe."

"Whoa, cool job," you say.

"It is," she says, with a smile. "It doesn't pay much. But I love it. So that makes up for it."

"What's the name of the troupe?"

"Dance the Night Away."

"I've heard of that," you say. "Maybe I'll come to a show."

"That would be great. We have a concert tomorrow night at the Dvorak Theatre. You could come."

"I'd love that."

"Awesome. If you wait around after the show, maybe we could grab a drink?" she suggests.

"I would like that," you say.

"Cool. See you then," she says, getting up.

[She uses a graceful exit and you have a time and place set up for meeting to talk again. A successful small talk conversation, no doubt.]

Example #4

You're standing in line at the coffee shop and run into a colleague who is an acquaintance. This is still small talk, but slightly different because you already know each other, so there are some ready-made conversation starters built into your relationship.

"Hey Cathy," you say.

"Hey, Dana. How are you?"

"I'm good. Glad it's Friday."

[The I'm good by itself wouldn't be a very interesting continuation of the conversation and might cause a stall. But adding that you're glad it's Friday is a Reveal and also gives her something else to respond to.]

"Yeah. I still have to go back to the office to finish some stuff up. You know, first, it's the phone, then the email, and then someone knocks at the door. Fridays and Mondays are really busy for some reason."

"Huh, interesting."

[She kind of hasn't given you anything to respond to here, so the conversation lags but doesn't quite stall as you recall something you can tell her which happened to you this week.]

"Well, it's been an interesting week in my office," you say. "There was a leak and I had to move everything."

"Oh no," she comments.

[And the conversation is back on track. A leak is interesting and there's plenty of conversational fodder.]

Example #5

There is a guy at your work holiday party that is super handsome and wearing the ugliest Rudolf sweater you have ever seen. You have been wondering about the strange juxtaposition of this hot guy in this terrible sweater all night and finally, you decide to be bold and use an ice breaker conversational starter and go ask him about the sweater.

"Hello," you say with a smile. "My name is Mercy."

You hold out your hand and he smiles back at you and shakes.

"Hey Mercy," he says.

"I have been wondering about your sweater all night," you say. "I must know where you got it."

[Reveal]

"It's sort of a long story," he says, his eyes twinkling. He *knows* the sweater is ugly.

"I must hear it," you say, wondering if you should say what you're thinking. You've had a couple of champagnes and you decide to go for it. "What is a good-looking guy like you doing in a sweater like that?"

[Encourage — asking a question that encourages him to talk about the sweater]

He raises one eyebrow when you say good-looking and is clearly pleased.

"It's because of Grammy," he says.

"Grammy," you repeat to show you're listening. "Got it. Go on."

"She knits these sweaters and she hasn't figured out that I'm not five anymore," he tells you, leaning in a bit, almost confidentially.

[SOFTEN — forward lean to show attention]

That doesn't seem to explain anything, and you prompt him to continue.

"So..."

"So today I stopped by my Mom's before the party and

Grammy was there with my Christmas present that she wanted to give me early because Mom had mentioned I was going to the party."

"Oh," you say, starting to get it.

"She wanted me to wear it." He looks a little bashful. "It's dumb. I know. And she wouldn't even probably remember that she gave it to me. Her memory's going."

This squeezes your heart a little.

"You could have taken it off when you got here. Before you came into the party. She wouldn't have known," you suggest.

He gives a little shrug.

"I promised her I'd wear it. And *I* would have known," he says.

Wow. Hot, loves his Grammy, and has integrity. The combination is almost too good to be true.

You *have* to ask.

"So, where's your girlfriend?" you say. "She must be around here somewhere!"

He gives a rueful smile.

"Nah. Girls don't go for guys in Rudolf sweaters," he says.

"They don't?" you say, pretending to think. "I could have sworn I did."

His eyes light up.

"You want to get out of here and grab a bite to eat?"

"Sounds great," you say.

Troubleshooting

Most conversations go well. But sometimes they don't. And it's important to think about what you'll do when things go wrong. This section is about common problems that you may encounter in any social situation where small talk is involved and what to do about them. We will discuss concrete actions that you can take if your conversation has gone off the rails. Maybe you can get it back on the track. Or maybe you need to just jump off. Either way, we have solutions for you, so that you are prepared when things don't go as expected.

Conversation won't start

Problem

You are attempting to talk to someone and get a conversation going and they don't seem interested despite your best attempts.

Possible causes

1. They just aren't interested in you because they think they're cooler than you.
2. The two of you just aren't a good fit.
3. You're doing something to turn them off.

Solutions

1. There's nothing you can do about them thinking they're cooler than you and not being interested. That's pretty much all on them. No matter what you do, they've already judged you and it's not likely they'll change their mind. Just move on.

2. Sometimes both of you are trying but you simply aren't a good fit. Again, be respectful and end the conversation, moving on to someone that you are more able to connect with.

3. It is possible that you are doing something to turn them off. So, you need to do a few checks.
A. Check your body language. Is it closed off and protective and you don't even realize it? Are you making eye contact? Are you smiling? Use SOFTEN to check the non-verbal cues you're sending.
B. When was the last time you heard them talk? Are you monopolizing the conversation? If you're not sure what their voice sounds like, then you're probably creating a conversational black hole for them and you need to stop. Ask them something about themselves. Use ARE or FORD to draw them out. Maybe you can revitalize the conversation by paying closer

attention and being interested in them.

C. Or are you asking too many questions? Possibly diving into topics that your conversational partner isn't ready for? Are you being weird? If you think in your nervousness you might have made some missteps in the conversation, then your best chance to salvage it is to come clean. Tell them you're a little nervous and that you're trying to improve your conversational skills. Be honest. If you're lucky, they'll understand and the conversation can start over with the ARE method.

If they're weirded out, though, you'll have to just politely excuse yourself and get out of there. Don't be hard on yourself about it though. Go to the restroom. Regroup. And try again. Remember to start easy with a shared experience. Then move on. There may be some eggs broken as you make this omelet. The thing is to not give up and keep trying. You'll get better at it the more you do it.

Conversation stalls

Problem

1. The conversation is coming to its natural conclusion. It's not actually a stall, it's an end.
2. The person you're talking to gives you a one-word answer and then neither of you says anything, causing the stall.
3. Your partner seems to have got bored and doesn't really want to continue talking to you because they aren't interested anymore, thus stalling out the conversation.

Possible causes

1. Sometimes you don't have much to say to a certain person. If that's the case, then respectfully end the conversation and move on. Neither of you has done anything wrong. There is a natural dynamic between two people and some have more to say to each other than others.
2. You've forgotten to ask open-ended questions and the person you're talking to has answered with a one-word answer. The conversation hits a brick wall and then you panic and don't know what to say.

3. You're not paying close attention to the person you're trying to talk to and you're not making sure they're interested in the conversation, so then you end up talking too much about yourself and the other person isn't interested in the topics you're trying to discuss.

Solutions

1. If you're just not a good conversational fit, then simply end the conversation respectfully and move on. No harm. No foul.

2. Remember to ask open-ended questions to begin with, and then you will avoid the conversational stall. Of course, at this point it's too late, so you can get the ball rolling again using the FORD method. Ask them a question about their family, occupation, or what they like to do in their spare time. The conversation is completely still salvageable and you may actually end up having a really good talk after a stall.

3. Again, try to avoid the stall that is caused by not paying attention to cues. But if it happens, then it's important to show that you are interested in the person and get them talking. Usually, this sort of stall happens when one person gets absorbed in their thoughts and starts what ends

up being a monologue instead of a dialogue.

This quickly gets boring for the other person.

So, the easiest way to end that sort of stall is to ask the other person a question about themselves or what they think of something. Everyone generally likes to talk about themselves or share their opinion, so it is sometimes an easy save for a real conversational faux pas.

Conversation partner gets glazed eyes

Problem

The other person's eyes have glazed over because their brain has gone into conversational overload.

Possible causes

1. You are talking too much about yourself or you are talking too much about something the other person isn't interested in.
2. You are talking too much about something the other person doesn't understand.
3. You are talking too much without letting the other person get a word in edgewise.

Solution

1. These ones are easy. Ask them something about themselves and stop talking about yourself and

your interests. You want to avoid being a conversational narcissist.

2. If the person showed interest in the topic at first, but then their eyes glazed over after a while, it could be for a few different reasons.

A. You're giving them too much information for a layperson who's unfamiliar with the subject.

B. You're possibly using jargon that they don't understand because they don't work or study in that field.

C. Or maybe they don't have the educational background to understand the concepts you're discussing.

In all cases above, just change the subject back to a more ordinary, less specialized, subject of conversation. Then learn from your mistake and give people less detailed explanations that give them a general overview but don't get too bogged down with concepts they may not understand. Making your conversational partner feel stupid is small talk suicide. Avoid doing this at all costs. If it means not talking about your specialization in quantum physics or your model trains, then so be it.

3. If you're talking too much in general, you're in danger of becoming a Conversational Black Hole and that's very bad. *Stop talking.* Listen instead. Become aware of your senses and

pay attention to the other person. Give the conversation some space to breathe. Let the other person share with you. You might just learn something new or make a new friend.

Conversation won't end

Problem

1. It's not a problem because you don't want to stop talking to this person. They're the most interesting conversationalist you've ever met.
2. Neither of you knows how to end a conversation.
3. You have been sucked into a Conversational Black Hole.

Possible causes

1. You've met someone fabulous. Great!
2. The conversation sometimes doesn't end because neither person can think of a way to end it.

Solution

1. No solution. Keep talking. Maybe you'll make a new friend.
2. This isn't good. You're stuck on the conversation-go-round. If you're both ready for it to be over, then someone needs to make the

first move and respectfully end the conversation. But maybe you can't think of any real reason to end it. If this is the case, then you can always say that you need to go to the restroom.

Then make sure that you really do go there. Never make something up because that's also small talk suicide and a really lame move. If you tell someone that you have to use the restroom and then you just go over to the bar when you leave them, that will be the worst thing ever. Just don't be a jerk and be honest and you'll be fine. If you need to go to the restroom because you need a reason to end the conversation, then so be it. Go to the restroom. Wash your hands or whatever. Regroup. And go out and try again.

Conversational black hole

Problem
You have been sucked into a Conversational Black Hole. Uh oh. This is the worst thing that can happen in a small talk situation.

Possible causes
In the case of a black hole, you usually haven't done anything wrong in terms of social rules. It's more bad luck than anything else. The other person is simply someone who can't stop talking and once they have a captive audience, they

just don't want to let them go.

Solution

It's important in this situation to remember to be respectful. This can be hard because you see everyone else having a better time than you and you really want to get out of the situation but there doesn't seem to be any way to extricate yourself.

First of all, give them a chance to talk but watch for any excuse to leave the conversation. Then, when you have given them as much time as you feel you can, use an authentic excuse to leave and respectfully do so. Use body language to indicate the conversation is over and past tense to show that you are done.

"It *was* great talking to you," you turn your body away from the person. "But I have to excuse myself. I really need to use the Ladies Room. It *was* good talking to you. Take care."

But what if they honestly barely stop for breath and you truly can't get a word in edgewise. Conversational Black Holes like this really do exist and once you get into their gravitational pull it is very difficult to get out. In this case, you'll have to actually interrupt them. Use body language to help show that you're ending the conversation.

Put your hand up, palm facing them — the sign for stop — and say, "I'm sorry, I'm going to have to interrupt you. I said I would help with setting up for the meeting and I really have to go. It *was* nice to meet you. See you."

Then turn and walk away decisively. Don't give them any reason to begin talking again.

Keep in mind that these people can't help themselves and its best to be understanding but not a doormat. You can let them talk for a while but then you need to leave the situation. Treat them with kindness and respect, the way you would want to be treated. Often these people don't have anyone who truly listens to them and that's why they try to make others listen to them by never stopping talking. We can be sympathetic and understand these people without allowing them to monopolize all our time

Conclusion

To conclude, small talk is a skill that can be learned. You can learn it. It takes some practice but you will get it. Remember to have a positive mindset and to pay close attention to the person and listen. You need to really be interested in the speaker and give them your complete attention because that is what a small talk master does.

But before you go out there and start chatting up a storm, bring your anxiety down to a manageable level using the breathing and 5 senses techniques. Make a good impression by practicing good hygiene, cleanliness, and make sure you dress appropriately for the situation.

Keep in mind that you are always communicating something. Even if you don't say a word. Use SOFTEN to remind yourself to use positive non-verbal behaviors to make yourself approachable.

Then it's show time and you're on. You are making small talk with an interesting person. Bring out the ARE method to get the ball rolling. Then move on to FORD. If you feel that you're making a good connection and your conversational partner is giving you cues they'd like to know you better, then you can deepen the conversation. But be sure that the other person is ready or else this can backfire.

End a conversation with grace and dignity, always

remembering to be respectful of the other person even if you didn't exactly hit it off. If you run into trouble, there's usually a solution. And the solution is usually to stop thinking so much about yourself and talking so much about yourself and let the other person get some airtime. Although, occasionally someone doesn't talk enough, and that is another problem altogether. Keep in mind the troubleshooting tips and you'll be alright.

It all comes down to treating a person right. Respect, honesty, authenticity, being genuinely interested in other people, and showing kindness is all it takes to become a small talk master. In this book, we have discussed many tips, tricks, acronyms, techniques, and methods. But what it really comes down to is being a good person and sharing yourself with another through words.

You can do that.

Everyone can.

Now go do it.

THE END

Your Opinion is Important to Me

First of all, thank you for purchasing this book. I know you could have picked any number of books to read, but you picked this book and for that I am extremely grateful.

If you enjoyed this book and found some benefit in reading this, I'd like to hear from you and hope that you could take some time to post a review on Amazon. Your feedback really makes a difference to me.

If you'd like to leave a review all you need to do is to go to the book's product page on Amazon and click on "Write a Customer Review"

I wish you all the best for your journey

Bibliography for Further Reading

ARE method
Dr. Carol Fleming (2013) t's the Way You Say It: Becoming Articulate, Well-spoken, and Clear. San Francisco: Berrett-Koehler Publisher

Four Ear Model
Friedman Schulz von Thun (1981) Talking to each other 1: Disturbances and Clarifications: General psychology of communication

FORD method
Practical Psychhology – www.PracticalPie.com

SOFTEN Technique
Don Gabor (2006) How to Start a Conversation and Make Friends, New York: Simon & Schuster.

McLean, S. (2005). The Basics of Interpersonal Communication (pp. 209- 210). Boston: Pearson

A and B. Wassmer, A. C. (1978). Making contact: A guide to overcoming shyness, making new relationships, and keeping those you already have. New York: Dial Press.

Cuny, K. M., Wilde, S. M., & Vizzier, A. (2012). Using empathetic listening to build relationships at the center. In E. L. Yook & W. Atkins-Sayre (Eds.)

Hogan, J. M. (2011). Public speaking and civic engagement.
Wassmer, A. C. (1978). Making contact: A guide to overcoming shyness, making new relationships, and keeping those you already have. New York: Dial Press.

About the Author

Diane always considered herself an introvert, but constantly strived to break out of her shy exterior. As she grew older, she put her mind to learning how to thrive as an introvert in an extrovert world, so she could tackle her shyness and no longer  fear the social situations she had grown accustomed to avoiding. This took her on a journey of studying all there was to know about communication and how it affects our everyday lives.

After completing her course in Communication and Media Studies, she embarked on a career as a public relations specialist in a Fortune 500 company. Now, although still an introvert, she no longer fears the social encounters that once held her back from living her life to the full. In fact, she now actually looks forward to them.

Today, she wants to share her journey to social freedom so that other people can learn to blossom in a world full of extroverts. Her desire to teach people how to become better communicators led her to write two books; an ultimate guide to mastering emotional intelligence, and an instruction manual on how to conquer small talk and become an expert conversationalist.

In her free time, she still enjoys learning everything there is to know about language and communication, but also always enjoys spending time with her family and being outdoors.

Made in the USA
San Bernardino, CA
29 November 2019